SO LONG, MARIANNE

A Love Story

by Kari Hesthamar

translated by Helle V. Goldman

ECW Press

SO LONG,
MARIANNE A Love Story

Published by ECW Press
2120 Queen Street East, Suite 200, Toronto, Ontario, Canada M4E 1E2
416-694-3348 / info@ecwpress.com

Originally published in Norwegian as *So Long, Marianne. Ei Kjærleikshistorie,*
Copyright © Spartacus Forlag AS, 2008
Norwegian edition published by Spartacus Forlag AS, Oslo
Published by agreement with Hagen Agency, Oslo
Lyrics to "So Long, Marianne," by Leonard Cohen, © Bad Monk Publishing, used with permission of Sony/
ATV Music Publishing and Scandinavia/Notfabriken Music Publishing AB.
All previously unpublished poems and other material by Leonard Cohen used with his permission.
The letters of Axel Jensen are quoted with permission of Prathiba Jensen.

Library and Archives Canada Cataloguing in Publication

Hesthamar, Kari, 1971–
[So long, Marianne. English]
So long, Marianne : a love story / by Kari Hesthamar;
translated by Helle V. Goldman.

Translation of: So long, Marianne : ei
kjærleikshistorie.
ISBN 978-1-77041-128-9
Also issued as 978-1-77090-501-6 (epub)
and 978-1-77090-500-9 (pdf)

1. Ihlen, Marianne. 2. Cohen, Leonard, 1934–. 3.
Jensen, Axel, 1932–. 4. Authors—Biography.
5. Hydra Island (Greece). I. Goldman, Helle
Valborg, translator II. Title.

CT1308.I55H4713 2014
920.72   C2014-900541-5

C2014-900542-3

Cover image: James Burke/Time & Life Pictures/
Getty Images
Photo on page 3: Jean Marc Appert
Photo of Helle Goldman by Jon Winther-Hansen
Photo of Kari Hesthamar by Maia Østerud (NRK)

Cover design: Tania Craan
Interior design and type: Rachel Ironstone

Printing: Friesens   1   2   3   4   5
Printed and bound in Canada

MIX
Paper from
responsible sources
FSC
www.fsc.org   FSC® C016245

This translation has been published with the
financial support of NORLA.

Canada

We acknowledge the financial support of the
Government of Canada through the Canada Book
Fund for our publishing activities.

CONTENTS

Come over to the window, my little darling,
I'd like to try to read your palm.
I used to think I was some kind of gypsy boy
before I let you take me home.
Now so long, Marianne, it's time that we began
to laugh and cry and cry and laugh about it all again.
Well you know that I love to live with you,
but you make me forget so very much.
I forget to pray for the angels
and then the angels forget to pray for us.
Now so long, Marianne, it's time that we began . . .
We met when we were almost young
deep in the green lilac park.
You held on to me like I was a crucifix,
as we went kneeling through the dark.
Oh so long, Marianne, it's time that we began . . .

Prologue

"LEONARD COHEN IS NO THIEF!"

"I had a very strange dream last night. For the last forty years of my life I've still been dreaming about Leonard. Even if he's together with someone else, and regardless of the setting, the dreams are positive for me. Last night he made another appearance and he says, 'Marianne, you must not talk so much.' And here I am sitting with you, looking at you, and you get me talking, talking, talking!"

That was my first meeting with Marianne. Spring was giving way to summer. She stood waiting for me by a narrow gravel road. "This was the beginning of my life," she said, spreading her arms.

We follow a flagstone path through an old kitchen garden the few metres down to the cabinlike wooden house. It is set on Marianne's maternal grandmother's property, just a stone's throw from where Marianne spent her childhood.

In the kitchen Marianne offers me warm slippers and Greek coffee. She switches between Norwegian and English when she speaks.

"It's strange when your life is linked to someone so well known. A magazine wanted to reunite me and Leonard at Fornebu Airport in the 1970s, when he was going to have his first concert in Oslo. The idea was to drive me out there in a limousine. The journalist camped out on my mother's doormat for twenty-four hours to get hold of me. I don't go in for that sort of thing. The distance of time has been important. It's easier to talk about these things now

than it once was. All the nonsense that's been written about us —
it's just pure fantasy. I haven't bothered to say how it really was."

"The story I always heard was that Leonard Cohen stole you
from Axel Jensen," I say.

"But Leonard is no thief! He's not a thief. Far from it."

Chapter 1

NINETEEN AND IN LOVE

A newborn girl is laid on the kitchen table in the big wooden house by the fjord. The older woman looks at the child, has longed to hold the girl, lifts her high in the air and exclaims, "You're finally here, my little princess!" The year is 1935 and Marianne is at her maternal grandmother's house in Larkollen for the first time.

When the war comes to Norway five years later it's safer in the countryside than in Oslo. The old woman has been waiting for her and takes her in as if she were her own. Marianne's mother has more than enough to handle with her little son and an ailing husband. Marianne returns to Larkollen, her childhood ahead of her. Back to the place where she felt she had been *seen* for the first time.

The older woman feeds the birds, which cautiously alight on her hand to eat. Time ticks by and Momo talks about being inside oneself, about being patient. When Marianne waves her arms in excitement the birds scatter in all directions. The old woman explains to the little girl what it takes to bring the birds to her hand. She says that it takes a long time to become so quiet that you can hear your own inner voice.

Momo tells fantastic stories, bearing away Marianne from their mundane lives on fabulous voyages. The automobile in the garage becomes a horse. Teaching Marianne to ride sidesaddle, her grandmother transports her to the land of princes, where everything has significance.

When Momo was little, she stood on a wooden crate in the back garden in Frogner, a well-heeled neighbourhood in Oslo, and sang for the neighbours. Later, when she began singing lessons, her teacher fell in love with the beautiful young woman. He was thirty years her senior. They were married, and the song was silenced. But still Momo sang for Marianne.

She sees and puts into words the ineffable. "I see and I know," says her grandmother. "You will meet a man who speaks with a golden tongue."

GENGHIS KHAN

Marianne is now nineteen years old and has just graduated from the Oslo Municipal Trade School. Lying in her room on Professor Dahl's Street, she writes in her diary and pines to be far away. When she was younger she read about Genghis Khan whenever she had a free moment. She had daydreamed about the ruthless Mongolian conqueror who ruled a kingdom stretching from the Pacific Ocean to the Black Sea. She imagined him embarking on expeditions, taking along his entire family and Marianne — his favoured wife, mother of many children. They thundered off with their horses and cattle, vanquishing new lands and erecting vast tented camps when evening fell. In her reverie, Marianne wore fluttering, brightly coloured garments and sat on horseback by the side of Genghis Khan, more than seven hundred years ago.

She still dreams that a handsome man will come and wrest her out of her ennui. Marianne closes her eyes and yearns. Yearns to be conquered and carried away.

Father would like her to become a doctor or a lawyer, but she's unsure about what to do with her life. She's studied business and taken a job as a secretary and general dogsbody at an attorney's office. Now, happily, it's Saturday night. The sun is still high in the sky, one of those days of late summer that seems as if it will last forever.

Laughter and lively voices issue from an open window. Marianne has been at a girls' party on Bygdøy Peninsula, an upscale suburb of Oslo, and now one of her friends wants to visit her boyfriend in the city. One of the girls has a driver's licence and has borrowed her father's car. The town rests sluggishly in the evening light. The laughing girls slowly make their way up Majorstua Street. And there stand four boys whose linked hands block the road. A suntanned boy sticks his head through the car window and looks at Marianne.

"Who are you?"

"My name is Marianne."

"You have to come to the party!"

And Marianne goes. Of course she does! They go to a party in a large apartment in St. Hanshaugen. Wearing a cardigan and green felt circle skirt she bought when she was an au pair in Newcastle, Marianne has padded her brassiere with cotton batting. The suntanned boy's name is Axel and he says that he has just come home from the Sahara. With slanted eyes and high cheekbones, he looks like a Mongol. He is rugged and sexy and blond. Marianne ends up sitting on his lap as he regales her with incredible stories from his journey in the desert. She has never met a man with so much to talk about, someone so entertaining. He talks about Theta and MEST — whatever that is — and everything is adventures and fables.

After the party breaks up, Marianne walks with light feet through the summer night. In a daze. She hasn't understood most of what was said, but she has been borne away on a journey. She knows that this moment could be the pivot on which her life turns toward an entirely new direction.

———

The year was 1954. The Theatre Café, the Engebret Café and the Lorry were artists' stomping grounds, where the modernists and more traditional artists engaged in heated debates. Literature began to concern itself with social criticism and the post-war consensus that established the modern welfare state of Norway. Axel was twenty-two years old and one of the emerging new voices, expressing ideas and thoughts that were strange to most people.

Spellbound by everything he said, Marianne was unable to get Axel out of her head after their first meeting. He was fascinating and knowledgeable and passionate about his ideas. Marianne had scarcely heard of the books and thinkers to which Axel referred. The home she came from could, at best, be characterized as bourgeois. Open to new ideas it was certainly not, and Marianne had wondered if this torpid, lacklustre existence constituted life. Now she hungered for the adventure that suddenly beckoned to her through a slender crack.

The day after the party in St. Hanshaugen Marianne went to Gothenburg, Sweden, for a friend's wedding. She had given Axel her telephone number on a piece of paper, and he had promised to call her when she came home. Some days passed before the telephone finally rang in the red brick house on Vestkant Square. They arranged to meet at Dovrehallen, a student pub with loyal regulars from diverse social strata.

Marianne had butterflies in her stomach, and her ordinarily unruly hair hung in soft blond waves after she had slept with curlers. She couldn't understand why people complimented her on her appearance. She thought her face was too round; all her life she had kept her eyes shyly downcast. Her first boyfriend had come over to her outside the Berle Girls' School and asked if she were looking for something. "Hi, have you lost something? I'm Beppe and I'd be happy to help you look."

Now she stood in her little room with the blue roller blinds and the writing desk so thoroughly plastered with pictures that the wooden top no longer showed under the glass. Her past shone back at her in small flashes: the first family portrait of her mother, father, brother Nils and Marianne. The class picture from the school in Majorstua, photographs of girlfriends, Momo's house, Marianne's first boyfriend whizzing down a hill on skis in a dark blue sweater with a white V-neck.

It was the room she retreated to when she was home. She often sat in bed eating crispbread with brown goat's cheese and drinking cold milk while she wrote in her diary. She kept her accounts in the little book, noting how much money she had used for the streetcar and the cinema. There were reports of parties and small, tightly written lines about her crushes and how she'd spent the day. From the window she could look across to Frogner Stadium, where she'd danced on skates. Inspired by the skating star Sonja Henie, Marianne had taught herself the figure eight, the arabesque and pirouettes. She swerved across the ice in a tiny skirt and brown figure skates passed on to her by her grandmother.

After skating Marianne would warm up in the changing room while she furtively read snatches of a mildly erotic pulp novel along with the other girls from Frogner. Along with Knut Hamsun's *Victoria*, one of the few books on her parents' shelves to capture her interest was Russian-American author Ayn Rand's *The Fountainhead*. It was the sexiest book Marianne knew and she'd worn out the covers reading it so many times. The protagonist, Howard Roark, went his own way and followed his own convictions — like Axel?

Dim light emanated from the ivory-coloured ceiling lamp. Mother and Father were making a din in the background. When she was little, Marianne used to sit beneath the heavy old bulbous-legged dining table while her parents quarrelled. She remained there silently, not even venturing out when she had to pee. Now she was a young woman whose heart thumped in anticipation of her date with a young man. Dressed in her finest clothes, she stood before the mirror in a red coat with a black velvet collar and matching cuffs, newly purchased from a secondhand shop. Waiting for her at Dovrehallen, at a small table with a red and white checked tablecloth, was Axel, smartly turned out in suit trousers and a shirt. A sparkle in his eye.

They chatted a while, kissed and became sweethearts there, that second evening together.

———

Marianne's father thought Axel was an interesting young man, but there was no getting away from the fact that he lacked education, employment and his own place to live. Her father had attended the Oslo Cathedral School and had a law practice and shipowners as friends, and it was among the sons of such people that he saw suitable marriage partners for Marianne.

Her parents' own marriage had caved in when the war came, bringing sickness and difficult financial straits. After contracting tuberculosis, Marianne's father spent a long time at the Mesnali sanatorium, just outside Lillehammer. There they burned away the upper part of his lung; later, during an operation to remove the lung, he barely survived a hemorrhage. Marianne's younger brother, Nils, then just two years old, had also suffered from tuberculosis for more than a year, wavering between life and death. Mother nursed her sick child and husband, and Marianne had been sent to her grandmother in Larkollen.

When the war had ended and they were all reunited, the family was not what it had been. Father's illness afflicted them all. Marianne imagined that her father silently demanded, "Pity me! Be kind to me! Don't contradict me!" Sickness made him unstable and he flew off the handle at the slightest provocation. Marianne was increasingly wary of her authoritarian father. The smile he'd once held at the ready had been ground away by the years of war and sickness. Before the war he had written lovely poems and been physically active; now he was gaunt and frail. He breathed so laboriously that he couldn't sprint for the streetcar when he was late. That had saved him during the war when the Germans bombed the streetcar that he should have been riding. Little remained of the man Marianne's father had once been.

As the 1950s wore on, Marianne's father lost his grip on his law practice — he lacked the lung capacity to carry him through an entire day in court. When the business suffered, Mother had to go out to work. Marianne's mother was the daughter of the prosperous opera singer Wilhelm Cappelle Kloed. She had been sent to Paris to learn French and had been among the first Norwegian young ladies to wear silk stockings. Now she was responsible for Nordland County at the licence office of the national broadcasting company. The north-country dialect jangled in her ears, but she did her best to handle the complaints from folks who rang from the far north. She came home tired in the evenings.

Marianne's parents were constantly picking on each other, but the underlying problems were never aired. Marianne's mother had taught her to put up with things, to grin and bear it. If she had to break a glass, take a mustard glass and not the crystal, said her mother.

———

After finishing at the Oslo Municipal Trade School, Marianne worked at various jobs and short-term positions — at the Kristiania Shoe Store, the cinema Norsk Bygdekino on Prinsens Street and, when the Russians crushed the Hungarian uprising of 1956, with the charitable organization Save the Children. To her it was all just temporary; she wanted something else but didn't know what. Life lay somewhere ahead, if only she could get hold of it and find a direction.

It was different with Axel. He wrote and wrote and knew that was what he wanted above all else. Without steady employment, Axel took whatever work he could find so he could put aside money for a journey he had in the back of his mind. In the afternoons and evenings he sat in front of the typewriter. He sent in short stories to newspapers and magazines and experimented with writing styles. Influenced by a touch of Hamsun and a little Hemingway, he sought his own voice in writing.

They spent their free time together, usually at Axel's place or other friends' homes. They played vinyl records and smoked cigarettes. On days with good weather they borrowed the sailboat that belonged to Axel's father and sailed in Oslo Fjord.

While Marianne dreamed about life out there, somewhere, the world floated before her eyes on the film screen. Like other young couples, they went to the movies and necked in the dark. At the Colosseum they saw *Boy on a Dolphin*, in which Sophia Loren and Alan Ladd make love in a windmill on the Greek island of Hydra. Filled with longing, Marianne snuggled close to Axel in the large movie theatre, wondering if she would ever find herself in such a beautiful place.

YOUNG AND INSECURE

Jazz blew in with the change in rhythm following the war. Axel was hooked on the new music, plonking on the piano and listening to all the latest from the USA. He played records for Marianne. Duke Ellington, Charles Mingus, Erroll Garner, Charlie Parker. Axel wanted to imbue language with that same rhythm, wanted what he wrote to be jazz. He tried to get Charlie Parker onto paper — jazz syncopation rendered in long squiggling sentences punctuated by some short ones. He had even handwritten a booklet about the history of jazz, systematizing musicians and instruments in illustrations and extended tables. Young Axel wrote that jazz, like eroticism, was a composite of primitive, elemental moods: grief, hate, melancholy, eroticism and joy merged into an entirely new spirit.

With Oslo's affluent West Side their home ground, Marianne and Axel belonged to a certain class and their social sets overlapped. The way the city was stratified, it was almost odd that they hadn't crossed paths before. In spacious apartments and houses in this part of town it was common to have home-alone parties, like the one Axel later wrote about in *Line*, published in English under the title *A Girl I Knew*, when Jacob enters the Bop Island villa among Oslo's well-to-do:

> Then we glided up a road with tall dark trees and stopped . . . A driveway brought us under an arch to a circle of grass with a fountain in the center, and around it there was a huddle of cars. Silent brutes with plated snouts and cold eyes . . . The muffled sound of jazz rose from the basement, silky-sounding, seeping in among all the furs hanging in the cloakroom.[1]

Marianne was in love, but being with Axel also made her insecure. They were so dissimilar; he was intense and loquacious, Marianne mild and unassuming. Axel was learned and intellectual, whereas she had stumbled into a universe of ideas that was completely alien to her. Feeling inadequate, she ploughed through the books that Axel prescribed for her — books he said would liberate her from the rules and norms of family and society and show her the way to her inner self.

Her parents were not unlike other parents in the 1950s, but Axel, who had come from a broken home, thought they were stiflingly conservative and strict. He took books to Marianne and jotted down titles of works he claimed would introduce her to ideas different from the middle-class notions that weighed her down. And Marianne read. Ouspensky, Nietzsche, Jung. She read page after page — she read just for the sake of reading. Word after word after word, but it wasn't her language and it didn't grab her the way it did Axel. The books didn't make the same profound impression on her as they did on him. There weren't many others in their circle of friends who read them either, but for Marianne understanding Axel became an obsession. She couldn't put her finger on what it was, but something in him resonated deeply within her. If the books and words became meaningful for her, would she gain a more equal footing with Axel?

Axel stood out from everyone Marianne knew. He wanted to be a writer and strike out in the world. He was his own man, liberated in a way she had never before encountered, always searching within himself.

The Theatre Café was their favourite haunt. Speaking with profound engagement about names such as Gurdjieff, Ouspensky, Jung and John Starr Cooke, Axel was the focal point of the table. Marianne listened and did her best to follow his soaring ideas. Sheer nervousness about not being able to keep up sometimes gave her migraines, occasionally sending her on a dash to the cellar to vomit in the toilet. On the first floor Axel sat and pontificated about philosophy. Their friends laughed and said, "Now Axel is way out in the Andromeda Galaxy again."

———

Axel had completed three years of high school in Frogner and wanted to enter university. But his encounter with the university was an affair that lasted just two or three days. Attending Arne Næss's lectures about preparing for entrance examinations, Axel found himself in a hall full of people who sat quietly and politely raised their hands. That was not his style. He decided to abandon the whole thing and instead do what his father had always thought was best: enter the family business and begin as an apprentice sausage-maker.

Axel shifted tins and lugged heavy sacks of salt, washed intestines and delivered products to restaurants. On one of the many uninspiring days in the steamy kitchen on Torg Street his clogs slipped on some innards and he skidded down the stairs to the cellar, where the carcasses were hanging. Landing with a bang at the bottom of the steps, he took it as a sign that enough was enough. He put an end to his sausage-making career that day.

Axel took up odd jobs again to make ends meet, writing in his free time. Marianne knew that he wanted to leave Norway. Oslo was like an old record spinning around and around and she also hankered to leave. Axel had a couple of pieces published in the newspaper *Aftenposten*, and sent in short stories to various magazines and journals. Most were rejected. On May 16, 1955, the short story "Yama" was politely but firmly returned from Johan Borgen, editor at the literary magazine *Vinduet*. Borgen wrote that "the mythic form rather obscures the message."

Several lengthier manuscripts were rejected, but in 1955, the year after he and Marianne had met, Axel debuted with his self-published book *Dyretemmerens Kors* (*The Cross of the Animal Tamer*). He had begun working on the surrealistic story when he was on his great journey through the desert and was living among the Tuareg people, where the men were veiled and barefoot. He arrived as a white man in a pith helmet and salmon-coloured boots, afraid of being bitten by scorpions and snakes. He eventually discarded the tropical helmet and acquired a burnoose and a donkey. He constructed a shelter of rocks and made a desk from a block of stone.[2]

Dyretemmerens Kors had the following foreword:

> How many people live in harmony with their inner
> myth? How many have some real experience that
> humdrum everyday life is the result of life's endless
> work with its organic material? How many are aware
> of the secretive symbolic language that their actions
> express? Who can read themselves between the lines?
> The answer must be very, very few. And precisely
> here lies the sinister sickness that is eating away
> at civilization, a creeping paralysis of the core of
> consciousness.

Axel went around to the newspaper editors in Oslo and enthused about his little book. He spoke passionately about dream symbolism, depth psychology and the unconscious, about Jung's analytical psychology and the relevance of Eastern thought for the Western individual. He was also very preoccupied with texts such as *The Book of Revelations*, *The Tibetan Book of the Dead* and the *I Ching* (*Book of Changes*).

Marianne went to her father's law office and tried to drum up sales among the staff. Axel peddled the novel at the slaughterhouse cooperative and to sausage-makers at his grandfather's factory. Together they traipsed around the Theatre Café and the Artists House gallery and sold the book to friends and acquaintances. The newspaper *Nationen* was one of the few to devote column space to it:

> Axel Jensen does not write for a popular audience, and his mystical language will probably not be understood or appreciated by many. But considered as an experiment the book is interesting, and it is a pleasure to meet a young author who is not following the herd.[3]

According to Axel no one had an inkling of what his book was about and in the end he burned the remaining copies.

———

Marianne seldom invited Axel or other friends home. She didn't want to introduce her friends to her parents, believing they weren't classy or intellectual enough for her social circle. Her brother, six years her junior, had gone through long periods of illness and was too young for them to have much in common. Her parents' troubled relationship cast a pall over the atmosphere in their home. They weren't pleased to have young people drifting in and out of the house, and Marianne quarrelled continually with her father. They clashed over curfew, homework and her choice of boyfriend. At the age of twenty, Marianne wasn't permitted to spend the Easter holiday with Axel and their friends at a mountain cabin. When Marianne's friends intervened on her behalf, her father remained adamant that only sluts went off like that. Her parents made Marianne think of the guards at the entrance to the royal palace; she imagined that they wore armour that shielded their hearts.

Axel was then living with his father in a part of Oslo known as Nordberg. Axel's father was remarried to a younger woman, and Axel had two young half-brothers. Axel wasn't on the best of terms with his father, who constantly reminded him that he lacked a job and his own place to live. In spite of that, it was more peaceful there than at Marianne's home. Axel had made a small den for himself in the house. He hung a red scarf across the window and lit a flickering candle for Marianne.

At the office in the morning, Marianne drew an arrow-pierced heart, inscribed "A + M" and accompanied by a greeting to her sleeping boyfriend:

> Yes, now your little wife is sitting at the office,
> plinking at the typewriter and thinking only of you.
> I love you more than anything on Earth, Venus,
> Jupiter, Mars, Saturn and all the worlds that don't
> exist. Take a good stretch and go into the bathroom,
> in the pocket of your new suit there's a little breakfast:
> buy fresh rolls, 1/3 of a litre of milk and something
> inspiring to put on the bread. Then wash your shirts
> until they're snow white and hang them to dry in the
> sunshine. Then you can do whatever you like, as long
> as you don't forget me for a single moment all day. I'll
> call you at 12:30 (or 1).

Marianne had become part of Axel's group of friends, and when they could afford it they went to the Theatre Café and ate sandwiches and pickled herring for the cheap price of 75 øre. But as a rule they met at someone's home every Saturday to share a bottle of Golden Cock gin mixed with orange juice and play jazz records.

Axel often became aggressive when he drank. Insisting on telling everyone how the world really worked, he wound up in heated arguments and fistfights. When she drank, Marianne felt that the alcohol freed her from herself — she just wanted to dance and disappear from herself and Axel's whims. She was good at pushing troublesome matters aside, and dancing made her feel weightless and happy.

Men noticed her and she knew that Axel was aware of it. But Axel didn't look upon her as merely a woman, as many other men did. He was convinced that the two of them could become something together. She too believed that. Axel wasn't frivolous: he wanted to lift her out of her prosaic existence and set her free — free just to be, without needing justification. But it wasn't easy to let one's light shine before others.

Sunday was the only day off work during the week, so Saturday was the big night for getting together. Three of their friends had single mothers and it was always open house at their homes. One of these belonged to Axel's friend Lasse, who lived on Bygdøy Peninsula. The house was called Bop Island, and would later become the model for the villa in Axel's book A *Girl I Knew*. Lasse was a considerate and dashing young man whom all the girls fell for, and his basement pad at the house was well suited for parties and the latest jazz.

———

It's one of many parties in the basement on Bygdøy. The talk is loud. People are dancing. Drinking. Discussing.

Nauseated and her vision blurring, Marianne feels the migraine pressing behind her eyes that comes when Axel philosophizes. Lasse escorts her up to the first floor, where his mother is, while the other young people continue the party in the basement. He shows her into a bedroom where she can lie down. Marianne curls up on the bed and rests her eyes. She is barely aware of the distant sound of the party down below.

Soon afterward she awakens with a jerk when the door is flung open and a drunken Axel barges into the room. He says nothing, just yanks her off the bed and hauls her by the arm into the kitchen. He looks at Marianne, lays his palm on the kitchen table, grabs a knife and drives it into his hand. Marianne hears the sound of the knife penetrating his flesh and bones. She closes her eyes. She hears the sound of the knife again. Twice. Three times. Sitting on a kitchen chair with her eyes closed, she hears loud voices in the room. *This isn't happening*, she thinks.

The blood flows. Someone fetches a towel and wraps it around Axel's hand. Marianne is sent home in a taxi, and Axel is tended by his friends.

Marianne was frightened by the incident but didn't talk to Axel about what had happened. She thought that if it could be just the two of them then all this would stop: Axel would settle down and the craziness would ebb away. But she would come to think of that small drama at the kitchen table on Bygdøy Peninsula many times later in life. She would replay the scene in her mind over and over again, asking herself why. Jealousy? She had more than once wondered if he was mad, this man she was with. He shaped her understanding of love, and on good days there was no other place she would rather be than with him. On these days anything was possible. But then came the times when he was volatile and bubbling with ideas that frightened her. Moments when he had a wild look in his eyes.

———

Axel used most of the day to write, going on short trips to work — his typewriter always in his suitcase. When he was away he wrote letters to Marianne about how he loved her and how she had to come quickly to him, or he to her. He sailed in regattas with his father's boat and loved to be on the sea. The buzz that sailing gave him was matched only by jazz.

In the summer of 1955 he went to the French Riviera to sail with Lasse. Marianne was in Oslo and received a series of longing letters. A small clover peeped green at her when she opened an envelope postmarked in the south of France:

JUAN LES PINS 3/8 – 55

Little one! Good one! Beloved!

The sun is baking, the waves are rolling and I love you. Today Lasse and I went out and sailed in the snipe, enjoying ourselves on the most gorgeous beach, with comfortable mats and the Mediterranean foaming under the soles of my feet. There's a great wind, and I love only, only you.

I've never been more disappointed than I was in Miel when there was no letter from you. I just hope you haven't changed your mind, that you've found your Superman that you've always been going around dreaming about. I want so much to be your Superman, to be your *Mofschen*, I want to hold you in my arms and kiss your eyes . . .

You must always love me, Marianne, never leave me. Perhaps we are among the few who can really be good together. We've fought, been crazy with jealousy and devilry, and always found our way back to each other — and that's where it's wonderful to be . . .

Darling, darling, Marianne. My yearning for you is indescribable. I often imagine that it's the two of us who are here in the Mediterranean. But the time will come. The whole future lies before us.[4]

Marianne was twenty years old and didn't know how right he was. She went to her job every day, happy to get out of the house. Her parents were terrified that she would fall pregnant by Axel, and for Marianne her home felt like a prison.

In spite of his declarations of love, Axel's feelings were unpredictable. He was impulsive and pursued his ideas in all directions. She hung back, or else tried to keep up, but both tactics were difficult. When she told him once that she was neither his mother nor his aunt, Axel retorted that he'd had more than enough of mothers and aunts in his life — he only needed Marianne. Full stop. Beautiful Marianne with her restless and imaginative mind.

Marianne had always had a rich fantasy life. She immersed herself deeply in her daydreams, imagining herself in scenarios ranging from film roles to the huge wedding she and Axel would have, attended by hundreds of guests. She shared her daydreams and night dreams with Axel, who listened with keen interest. When he was away, she wrote him letters with accounts of what had come to her in her sleep. *A book in a display window. Rita Hayworth's typewriter. An argument with her father.*

She had long wished to create something herself, and she fantasized about standing on the stage, where she could put herself in someone else's place and live out that role in front of an audience. When she was small, Momo told her a story about how she once travelled all the way to China to marry an ambassador. The journey by sea took many weeks and when she arrived the young man had died. He had been run down by a horse and carriage, but her grandmother stayed in China for several months.

Marianne had listened to the dramatic tales with round eyes. She had lived with Momo for most of the war, and on cold winter nights they had shared a bed. Momo always spread Marianne's clothes under her so they would be nice and warm when they arose in the morning. Sometimes they just lay there, the new person and the old one, listening to the wood crackling in the iron stove and sharing what they could remember of their dreams from the night.

Now Marianne had turned twenty-two, and she wished she could go to her grandmother for advice. Momo had died shortly after Marianne had met Axel so she sought out her mother's cousin, an actress who had helped establish the National Academy of Theatre in Oslo. Marianne read Ibsen's *The Wild Duck* with her until tears ran down her face. She studied the role of Hedvig and after rehearsing the part she decided, with the support of her mother's cousin, to take the academy's entrance examination — to her parents' intense despair.

Beset by resistance at home, Marianne lost her nerve and in the end didn't take the exam.

THE RIGHT PATH

Marianne often told Axel that she was afraid of being alone, always apprehensive that he would abandon her because she wasn't interesting enough for him. Her fear intrigued him and he reminded her of it incessantly:

> The fear of being alone is a foretaste of what lies
> beneath that youthful fragrant wonderfulness. The
> angst is within you, and you should tend it. Behind
> it lies buried something substantial, you can be sure
> of that. I know that these bugbears of which I so
> often speak tend to irritate you. But your irritation
> tells me that you are still inexperienced. Find the sun
> behind the angst. We will eventually have a language
> in common. Later we will speak more of the same
> language.[5]

Axel wanted Marianne to seize hold of what she dreaded and hold it up to the light. In this way she would more easily achieve self-realization and liberate the powers within her.

I am so certain that something creative dwells within you. Every person should create something. We are here on this Earth not to sleep but to create. The act of creation is the most important in life and when all is said and done it is the only thing that gives existence some kind of meaning. To create is to see one's own being deposited in the things outside of ourselves. When you create you share yourself with other human beings. He who does not create is self-contained. He encapsulates himself, congeals. What is life for an eating, shitting and sleeping animal? Life has given us a brain and senses to use for something! To create! And YOU! You can CREATE!

It's just a matter of finding a form of expression. Energy and strength are boiling within you, searching for a form. Those dreams of yours, my God. I've been saying for a long time that a creative power lives within you. It's not a question of world fame. The joy is in the act of creation itself. It's a true joy, Marianne.

I write because I must. Without creating existence loses all meaning. I write because I must release my mind of something that is pressing to come out . . . My self is my only motive. I love you, Marianne. I could do everything for you. But you must live your own life. I can't live your life for you. I can't create for you either. You must work all this out for yourself. One can't do anything for someone else. One can't know what is best for another person, deep down. How would one know? One doesn't even know oneself.[6]

Axel believed that one of the reasons he was drawn to Marianne was that she was more grounded than he. Moreover, he had never allowed himself to be attracted to insignificant people for any length of time and was therefore certain that a powerful force lived within her. He thought that he could unshackle her from the surface, while Marianne would root him in the earth. In this way they complemented and empowered each other.

Marianne was boundlessly in love with Axel and for her his letters weren't didactic or moralizing. What he wrote appealed to her, and Axel's view of life and humanity represented something new and free in which she desired to be included. But they had their conflicts. Axel was so overbearing that Marianne often disagreed with him just so he would notice that she was there. Axel thought that she was all at sea; she was wrong whether she expressed an opinion or kept quiet.

Marianne was about to awaken as a young person, and Axel, who was both exciting and incomprehensible, aroused her sexuality. At the same time he offered her a new way of looking at herself and made her understand that there were other ways of living. Axel could take her away from her parents and their bourgeois expectations. The thought of a free life beyond the behavioural strictures of Oslo's West Side both enticed and frightened her.

Even though Axel represented freedom from home and her quotidian existence, the freedom didn't offer her a secure framework. Something painful and bitter frequently arose between them, supplanting their love for each other. Axel often lost control of his temper. Very few people understood what preoccupied him and he often felt lonely. Marianne felt a frisson of fear about what she had gotten herself into — there was so much that was different about Axel — and occasionally she thought that he was utterly without limits. But the young lover steadily insisted on guiding her along the path toward inner and outer freedom.

Think for yourself now, my own little woman, when
you've purchased a dress or a pair of shoes. Then
you're bursting to tell me. It means something to you,

and you want so much for it to mean something to me too. That's the way it is for me too. Because something extraordinarily important is happening through my person. Understand me right. It's not me as a person that's important, but something that's happening inside of the person, I am beginning to get down to something of the gem.

. . . Do you remember all the tiny turtles? How they hatched and how they began to run down toward the shore. On the way many were eaten up by birds. Only a few survived and made it to the ocean, to the water. There even more were eaten by fish, and perhaps some few grew up and became large. Just a few managed to carry out the program of their lives. The others were consumed by life. Their forms disappeared. They disintegrated in the stomachs of birds or fish. Became the flapping of wings or the gentle movements of tail fins. But the original idea, to become a turtle, was not realized. That could only happen in the great depths. That is essentially man's place in the universe. Just a few of us reach the edge of the water, the place where the spirit can be nourished. Just a few of us accomplish our goal and become Human, far too many become something else, something used up by life, something that is equated with life. But when we come down to the great depths. Then the world is still and clarified . . .

I want so much to be your sustenance, to be your light and your water. That's why I'm often seized by bitterness when I see that instead I'm the person who makes you desperate, chaotic, confused and unhappy . . . My own wonderful turtle, I feel and I hope that you have this something extra in you that can open your eyes so that you can see the ugly vampire that sits on your back, that creature in yourself that empties

you of nourishment. And when you begin to suspect
something of this . . . this unknown power that is
fed by your negative emotional life will withdraw,
the devil will lose his interest in you and God will
redouble his.

Forgive me this letter. I love you.[7]

JOHN STARR COOKE

Marianne kept Axel's letters in a drawer in her writing desk
and read them over and over in the dim light. She curled up on
the bed in her light-blue pyjamas, closed her eyes and tried to
envision Axel.

In 1955 Axel was in Copenhagen for some weeks with the
mystic John Starr Cooke. When Axel was deep in the Sahara
the bizarre man had appeared, riding a white camel. Cooke was
dressed in a black burnoose and didn't have a hair on his head.
He told Axel that he was an incarnation of Pharaoh Amenhotep
the Fourth and that he had met both Gurdjieff and Ouspensky.
Everything that Axel had been so absorbed by had materialized
before his eyes when he encountered Cooke in the desert.

Cooke came from one of the wealthiest families in Hawaii
but had chosen to devote his life to occultism instead of the
family businesses. One evening John had the idea that he and
Axel should swing a pendant over a map and travel together to
wherever the pendant stopped. The pendant came to a standstill
over the town of Øksfjord in Finnmark, Norway's nothernmost
county. It was simply a matter of leaving the Sahara and turning
their noses northward.[8]

But now John had wound up in the hospital in Copenhagen,
paralyzed from the waist down. John believed that his condition
was linked to an insect bite he'd received in Algiers. Travelling
to Denmark to be there for his old friend, Axel wrote letters full
of desire to Marianne back in Oslo.

Marianne smiled a little at her mental picture of her boyfriend at the hospital with John, Axel pounding away on his Remington typewriter. She didn't wait long before she took out pen and paper and answered:

> It's horrible to be alone, darling. Everything is so strange, why am I never content with anything? Peculiar thoughts rush through my head, making me uneasy and sad. When Father says something I can scarcely keep myself from flying into a rage. Darling, you are used to me and my whims, but it's true that I have pains in my head, in all of me. Darling, you are the only one who can help me. You say that it is only me who can help myself. Yes, yes, that must be true. But God knows where I'll begin. Fear of not being able to reach (follow) you drives me crazy. I am so wonderfully in love with you, proud of you. You mean so damn much to me.
>
> Poor John, he must be in a bad way. I should be ashamed for complaining. He surely needs you.[9]

Marianne had met John some months earlier, soon after he was admitted to the hospital in Copenhagen. She had gone with Axel to visit him, and had looked at him with a pitying gaze and said she felt sorry for him. "Cut that out," he had responded brusquely, "It's no help!" He had asked her to go to the woman in the next room. There lay a twenty-six-year-old woman who had been injured in an automobile accident just after she had been married. Now she was bedbound, trying to write down her thoughts with a pencil clamped between her teeth.

When Marianne left Copenhagen John had given her a gold bar that had filled her clutch bag. Earthly goods were of no interest to the mystic from Hawaii, who had asked her to sell the gold bar and put the money in her bank account. She boarded the

33

Danish boat with half a kilo of gold under her arm and deposited it in a safety deposit box when she got to Oslo. The bar wasn't numbered but she and Axel checked that it was the real thing.

"WE MUST GET MARRIED"

In 1957 Axel was called up for military service. Meeting at the Theatre Café the evening before his departure, they kissed and said goodbye for a year. Axel joked, "I'll meet you after work tomorrow," but Marianne was prepared for a long separation from her lover.

The next day, when she came out of the office Axel was waiting, in his duffel coat. He had talked his way out of military service and come right back to Oslo the same afternoon. To celebrate his homecoming they went straight to the Theatre Café, where they found the usual gang. Duffel-coated Arne Nordheim sat, as always, at his own table. Judge Einar Moen was there, and Axel's good friend Per Schioldborg.

Per had been with Axel in the Sahara in 1953. Axel, Per and his girlfriend Else Berit had travelled by train to Nice, where she stayed behind while the other two hitchhiked and travelled in smugglers' vehicles through the land of the Tuaregs, to Tamanrasset and the Hoggar Mountains, which was the goal of the journey. Per returned to Nice after a few months; he missed Else Berit and wanted to go back. Axel gave himself over to solitude and his own reflections. Surrounded by thousands of miles of sand, he had fixed himself up with a stone shelter and begun on a novel about his great passage through the desert. He wrote about craving insights other than those supplied by the established elite. He wrote about the fabulous and the supernatural.

Axel had always been drawn into the most remarkable adventures. Now he had begun again to think about travelling to a place he had never been before, and he wanted Marianne with him. The time for lazy daydreams was past. Marianne, whose travels beyond Norway had been few and safe, fantasized about the romantic departure they would make. They both began to put aside money for the trip. Axel was grappling with his first novel for Cappelen, one of Norway's oldest publishing houses, hoping it would add a little money to the pot.

On a writing excursion to the village of Øyenkilen, outside Frederikstad, he sat before the typewriter and related that the writing proceeded slowly. The individual sentence itself posed no difficulty, the challenge was getting the whole thing to hang together, to create an undertone and a sense of coherence throughout the book.

But now he wanted them to marry! He wanted to take Marianne away from the environment that he believed destroyed something in her, day by day, and that he claimed would break her down.

> I don't mean in any way to set you up against your
> own parents, but the climate in your home is perilous
> for a soul that wants to come up. I can't comprehend
> how you hold out, that you don't explode and fly off the
> handle, I can't comprehend how you can be so sweet
> and good to me, so difficult and jealous and devilish as I
> can often be. But I'm sure that everything will be fine
> if we marry and get away from the whole mess.
> We'll get engaged on the twentieth of May. It will
> be a shock for them . . . It isn't out of fear that I don't
> ask your father, but because to a certain extent it's
> repulsive to give him a say in this matter. Why should
> I ask him? It's you I want! It is you I ask. So forget
> about the old formalities. They are so easy to see
> through anyway. If they don't think I'm good enough,
> how much that reveals of their innermost souls! Just
> because I'm not loaded. Just because I'm a person who
> has something to live for, who has something that

lifts him a bit above the grey masses and blows a little sunshine into life, just because I refuse to take things exactly the way they are, refuse to follow the same old tracks and sniff along like a dog, just because I want to create my own future and my own home as *I* would like it, not as others say I should have it nor what they say is proper and fitting.[10]

Axel wanted to share his life with Marianne, to become something together with her. But it mustn't happen at the expense of either his soul or hers. The more he thought about it, the more evident it became to him that even though one shouldn't ride roughshod over others, at the same time one had a duty to one's self and one's own soul. He made it clear that marriage with him would rip Marianne out of her old rut. They wouldn't have much "dough" but it would be exciting:

I shall whirl you into a world that is new and alien to you and that is necessary for you to dissolve all the old corpses that are sloshing around in your brain. Come out into the fresh air and become human! It's a fucking planet we live on, not a neighbourhood or a miserable little town in the far north. Whether you plant the seed in Norway or Spain it becomes a plant, right? Yes, I dare say that the strong sun and the cloudless sky offers a greater margin of happiness than the leaden Oslo Fjord on a chilly winter's day. One gives up something and receives the sun in return. And the sunshine is always accompanied by clear-cut shadows. I like clear-cut shadows. I like them endlessly more than this dull grey ingrown milieu that has lost all meaning for me. We must get out, Marianne. We weren't born for this. No, no, careful now. I'm not turning my back on Norway. But I'm

not a Northman, I'm an Earthman. I live on a planet.
And the planet is sailing through space. What is Oslo?
A speck. A moaning dust mote. And the forests here
in the north are so cold, so cold.[11]

Marianne thought that Axel could make her complete and
fill the longing in her. There was something about his voice,
the intensity of the words that issued forth from him. He spoke
with enormous authority and always took things further than
anyone else, enthusiastically breaking boundaries and bearing
his companions out of the commonplace. Marianne couldn't
count the times she had heard him exhort, "You mustn't stop
there!" when someone raised his voice or threw himself into the
discussion around the table.

He was like a preacher; he was without a doubt one of those
people who seemed to know what made the world go around.
When Axel came into her life, she wanted to let go of everything
— her family, her own identity. But at the same time she was
petrified. She was like a bird flapping with one wing while the
other wing hung down uselessly. The freedom that waited for her
out there was simultaneously tempting and oppressive. She feared
losing control over her life and wished that Axel were more
grounded. She was afraid of not being up to tackling the new life
that they contemplated. She bridled when anyone — her family
or Axel — tried to lead her. Equally she felt lost when he wasn't
there and wrote back to him as soon as she received his letters.

In a strange way it's beautiful, but it also scares me
that I would be so lost without you, Axel. I miss you,
I must see you, hear your voice. You are mine. I read
all your letters yesterday. The one from Øyenkilen
and the one about the turtles, and every time I read
them, I feel more and more what you mean, see it
so damn clearly, if I could just really hold on to it

and follow through. I have seen the vampire that
sucks sustenance from me, so now it's just a matter of
getting rid of it.[12]

Full of youthful insecurity, she wrote back to Axel in his own
language and pretended she was tougher than she really was. But
she was unable to put his advice into practice in her daily life or
ask herself the question "What do I want to do with my life?" It
was Axel who steered the relationship and she understood that
if she wanted to be with him their life together would be mostly
on his terms. Marianne knew that if she joined him an adventure
was in store for her that few others could offer her. He was her
Genghis Khan.

It was Axel who had invited her to dance and she tried her
utmost to follow the jazz rhythm. His keynotes would not change,
but perhaps hers could.

———

Axel suggested in one of his letters that they should write
travelogues together. He promised to help her with the genre
until she got the hang of it and then they would submit the
manuscripts under Marianne's name. They would use the money
for something they both needed — a new typewriter for each
of them. Marianne wrote in her diary almost daily, filling the
small notebooks from cover to cover. Nothing ever came of the
travelogues.

IKAROS

In the middle of planning their big trip abroad came Axel's
explosive breakthrough as an author. In 1957, when Axel was
twenty-five, Cappelen published his novel *Ikaros* and he was
declared a genius by Norwegian book reviewers. The story
described a young man's journey through the Sahara. At a deeper

level, the novel concerned a thirsting for the fabulous and the supernatural and a quest for experience and one's bearings in the world. In the magazine *Vinduet*, the literary critic Kjøv Egeland wrote that not since Knut Hamsun had a Norwegian youth stood out in Norwegian literature with greater determination and a greater claim to be different. "Here is one of the year's most sensational works of fiction. Sumptuously rich, brightly talented, fascinating," opined Egeland. In short order, *Ikaros* was reviewed in more than thirty Norwegian newspapers and Axel and the book were lavishly praised by the critics.

Axel was interviewed everywhere. Cappelen's head, Henrik Groth, staged a press conference so journalists could meet the young man, who talked about the book and his travels in Europe and Africa. There was a reception at Cappelen and dinner at the grand home of Groth and his wife on Bygdøy Peninsula. With a view over the fjord, the house boasted columns and one drawing room after the other. Marianne felt as if she were at a palace ball. She stood aside and watched while Axel was borne aloft on the wings of his success.

———

Marianne and Axel wanted to go south — to Greece. Planning to root his next novel in the Oedipus legend, Axel sought the mythological atmosphere of the Mediterranean coast. He intended to rent a house, where he would have peace and quiet to write the book. Marianne had been in Denmark and had worked as an au pair in England, but more extensive travels she had only taken in her imagination and through the stories told by her grandmother and Axel. Now Axel wanted to take her to a country he hadn't visited before. Marianne thought that everything would be simpler there. It would just be him and her. Axel would find contentment with her and with his writing.

She didn't tell her parents of their plans. She knew they would oppose them, and she dreaded raising the subject.

In the summer of 1957, Marianne is staying at the home of her
mother's cousin, looking after the children while their mother
tours the country with a theatre production. One evening,
Marianne asks her friends Lasse and Unni to babysit for her while
she goes to meet Axel at the Theatre Café. Marianne rides the
streetcar downtown and at the café Axel is waiting for her at
a small round table near the bar. Seated at his right is a young
woman with long black hair. Axel introduces the two women to
each other, and Marianne takes the empty chair beside the woman.
Marianne tries to read Axel's face; she knows how feelings can
flit like clouds across his face, the way a small child shifts from
laughter to anxiety in seconds. She thinks his smile looks like a
grimace when he turns toward her and opens his mouth:

"I'm leaving for Egypt with this woman tomorrow. There will
be no trip to Greece."

Marianne feels as if she's been struck. She overturns the heavy
chair behind her and storms out, running as hard as she can up
Storting Street and turning left toward the Scala Cinema. Her
heart pounding, she comes to a halt in front of the glass showcase
advertising films, which shines toward her. In desperation,
Marianne stares ahead of her, preparing to smash her face into
the pane of glass, but as she tips her head backward a hand stops
her. Axel spins her around and takes her by the hand.

Without a word he leads her across the street and strides to
a taxi stand behind the National Theatre, puts her in a car and
instructs the driver to take her to 1 Kirke Road at Frogner Place.
Axel pays the fare and tells Marianne that he'll follow later.

"It's going to be okay, Marianne!" he says.

Lasse and his girlfriend exchange glances when Marianne
staggers through the door.

"That guy isn't worth it," they say, and wrap her in a blanket on
the sofa. They fill a glass with red wine and stroke her back while

she relates what's happened. Marianne talks until she is hollow and falls asleep, exhausted.

At four o'clock in the morning the doorbell awakens her. Axel is standing on the steps, grinning.

"We're going to Greece! It's you I want to travel with!"

———

Marianne's parents thought going to Greece with Axel was an appalling idea and did their best to talk her out of it. Yes, Axel was charming and intelligent, but more than that they were not willing to credit him. The young writer was a very bad risk. They weren't even married, and what were Marianne's parents supposed to tell the neighbours — that she'd run away? Marianne felt that it was now or never: if she didn't board the ship it would sail without her.

She had made up her mind. Some weeks later she and Axel had saved enough money to make their way through Europe to Athens. They could pack their bags, ready to leave Oslo behind.

Chapter 2

AWAY FROM NORWAY

It's a Wednesday evening in mid-November. Professor Dahl's
Street lies in near darkness, weakly illuminated by a solitary
lamppost and yellow light from the neighbours' windows. Father
sits in the green chair by the radio when Marianne goes out the
door, suitcase in hand. He doesn't quite believe it when she
says she's leaving. Mother has just gone to a meeting. Her last
sentence before the lock clicked behind her was, "If you need
anything, you know where I am." No hug, nothing.

Marianne is miserable. There is nothing she desires more than
to go away with Axel, but it's hard for her to leave against her
parents' wishes. It's occurred to her that her father will give up
playing bridge to avoid being asked about Marianne and having
to say that his daughter has done a runner out of the country. She
has lain awake thinking about the shame she is bringing them.
And how will her brother Nils — now alone with their parents —
fare after her departure?

Axel's entire family — relatives of all ages — have trooped into
Central Station to say goodbye. They kiss and embrace and wave
from the platform. Marianne is alone but as she's about to board
the night train she sees a familiar face. Her father is standing by
one of the station's handsome old columns. He has hopped on
the streetcar to reach her before the train departs. Marianne runs
to him and throws her arms around his neck. Father asks where

Mother is and says he wonders why she isn't at the station to send off her daughter. Marianne doesn't know. Father looks at her and says that she ought to have given him a hug before she left. Marianne is glad that he asks about her mother, something he never does. Now she thinks that after she's gone life may be easier for her parents, without her to worry about.

Axel sits in the train compartment and waits. They're bringing no more than they can carry. Some clothing. Axel's typewriter and a supply of food for the soul: Gurdjieff, Ouspensky, Henry Miller. Snorre, Bjørneboe and Ibsen. Jung and Nietzsche. Marianne is wearing a fur coat inherited from her grandmother. Unable to stop the tears after parting from her father, she sniffles her way to Germany. Setting out on the path to personal freedom is no walk in the park.

During an interview the previous day Axel said that he viewed travel as an internal process. He didn't believe in writers who live in pleasant suburbia and write pulp fiction about Oslo's sordid backstreets. No, a writer must launch himself out into the greatest depths and not simply allow written words to substitute for living himself.

Together with Marianne he bids farewell to the motherland. They plan to be away for one year. With luck, he'll have a new book ready when he returns home.

———

In Hamburg they took lodgings in an old attic room with a slanting floor, sleeping under a big warm duvet on the beautiful bed. They spent a few days there looking for a car. When Axel bought a secondhand blue Volkswagen Beetle, they headed south again. Marianne had dried her tears and found some peace of mind. Piling their earthly belongings into the car, they drove through shifting landscapes and slept in the Volkswagen or in cheap accommodations along the way. It was uncomfortable and romantic.

Axel had introduced Marianne to the dream interpretations of Carl Gustav Jung and was engrossed with the analytical psychology of the Swiss professor and with the relation between the individual's conscious and unconscious energy. He got the notion of stopping in on Jung on the way to Greece. They drove into Zurich, strode into the legendary C.G. Jung Institute and — willing to give anything a shot — asked if they could meet with Doctor Jung. They were granted ten minutes with Jolande Jacobi, who ran the centre together with Jung. They were informed that, regrettably, it was impossible to meet the great man without an appointment.

They carried onward to a cold and rainy Venice and from there south to Rome. Marianne called the trip their "honeymoon," and Axel bought her an orange shirt-dress with a tie-belt and buttons up the chest.

From Italy they went to Yugoslavia. Stopping in Skopje, in Macedonia, they beheld the half-finished square brick houses around them. Marianne had the impression that they had driven onto the stage of an old film in which she and Axel had accidently been given the lead roles. She was struck by the contrast between the poverty there and the comfort of the Norwegian life they had both come from.

The streets were decorated with photographs of President Tito, whose face — dangling in long garlands — gazed down at them. Food was scarce. Marianne and Axel went into a newly built supermarket with a ceiling supported by tall, majestic pillars, at the feet of which were old-fashioned spittoons. Sparsely stocked shelves stretched toward them. There were just some biscuits and bread to be had.

During the last stretch from Yugoslavia into Greece, neither of them was aware how dangerous it was to drive with summer tires over those wild mountains. They twisted and turned their way down the foggy mountainsides. All of a sudden, the little blue Beetle spun around 180 degrees on the thin layer of ice, slamming into one of the boulders that served as a crash barrier. The car came to a stop with its nose facing the precipice. Fear hammered in their temples. Axel sat with his hands on the steering wheel and glared furiously down the misty valley. They cautiously opened the doors. No sooner had their feet touched the ground than it slid out from under them and they both lay floundering on the icy road.

With considerable effort they manoeuvred back into position on the road. Returning the way they had come was impossible so they were forced to proceed downward. Night had fallen by the time they had navigated their way down the steep mountain and found themselves in the Greek countryside. No street lights, just Marianne and Axel alone on the country road, rattling along in their blue Volkswagen with its yellow headlights, like a small insect creeping slowly forward. A few Spartan houses rested in the night, reminding them that there was life out there.

In a godforsaken place near Thessaloniki, Axel stepped hard on the gas pedal and the car responded with a cough, rolled slowly along the road — the motor dead — and was swallowed by the night's silence. From the car Axel and Marianne could see golden light shining from the window of a shepherd's hut. They walked over to it and carefully knocked on the rough wooden door to the whitewashed stone house. An elderly couple with a half-grown boy received them with open arms and loud voices. They embraced them and gesticulated and said lots of things that Marianne and Axel couldn't understand.

It appeared that the old couple and their grandson were staying there to look after the family's sheep. The little dwelling consisted of one room with an earthen floor, a bed in the corner and a kerosene lamp, which shone in the night's darkness. The battered wooden table was set for four. Marianne wondered who the fourth plate was for, not yet knowing that it was a Greek custom to put out an extra place setting in case an unexpected guest arrived.

The old man and woman offered what they had. Marianne and the woman shared the simple bed, lying side by side in their nightgowns on the straw mattress. The three men bedded down on the floor for the few hours that remained before dawn.

The next day Axel hitchhiked to Thessaloniki, where he managed to get a mechanic to come back with him to look at the car. After thanking the little family that had taken them in so hospitably and waving goodbye, they made it to Thessaloniki by driving with the choke on. After the Beetle was repaired they made their way south over the mountains. They were in high spirits — the car was working like new and they made good progress.

Just before a left turn, Marianne is stabbed by a sharp pain and lets loose an ear-piecing howl. As she screams, two women — dressed in white and donning headdresses marked with red crosses — materialize in front of the car. Marianne looks in astonishment at the women. Convinced that she's gone to heaven and is flanked by white angels, she shouts, "I'm dying!" Axel slams on the brakes and leaps out of the car.

The women are nurses from a nearby hospital, out with a patient in a wheelchair. Realizing that Marianne is in pain, one of them climbs into the car while she fishes a small bottle of smelling salts out of her pocket and inserts it into Marianne's nostril. The nurse directs Axel around the bend and onward to a large white house. A German-speaking doctor pronounces that Marianne's appendix is about to burst. He asks if they would like the operation done there or if they would prefer his private hospital in Lamia, the next village. Marianne thinks, *Private is much better!*, and is carried into the car. After a short ride they come to an old stone house where the shutters swing on their hinges like in a Bela Lugosi horror film.

Marianne is borne in and placed on an old iron bed. The nurses hang up a sheet so she can't see beyond her waist during the operation. Standing by her head, three black-clad Greek women pray for her, their torsos rocking while they mutter incomprehensibly. The nurses catch flies with their bare hands, releasing the buzzing insects out the window. Marianne hears low voices through her fog of pain. Seated beside her in the big white room, with its stone floor and peeling paint, Axel — meek and pale — holds her hand. Marianne screeches. Shrieks with all her strength, in German: *"Schmertzen Doktor, Schmertzen Doktor!"*

Marianne is to receive local anaesthesia for the emergency procedure. When the nurses come with a lethal-looking syringe that seems big enough for a horse, Axel tumbles off his chair and sinks to the floor. The nurses hoist the limp man to his feet and convey him out of the room. The next thing Marianne remembers is feeling the knife slicing into her abdomen.

———

Marianne is in the hospital for a week and Axel stays there with her. While Marianne lies in bed with a moist wad of cotton in her mouth and recovers her strength after the operation, Axel has taken out his typewriter and is writing like a madman. Every time he doesn't like what he's written, he crumples up the sheet of paper and tosses it in the rubbish bin or on the floor. Marianne hears the familiar sound of fingers pounding on the keyboard and thanks God for this shred of their old life. And she's alive! Recovering slowly, she begins to look forward to getting on the road again. The nurses marvel at the foreign couple: guests from so far away don't come every day.

About twenty-four hours after the operation Marianne drags herself to the toilet for the first time. She takes small steps along the drab corridor to the toilet, which consists of a hole in the floor. On the dingy stone wall small squares of paper are speared by a nail. Marianne takes a paper from the nail and squats down. Looking at the paper, she recognizes Norwegian words and sentences on the grey-white paper. The nurses have neatly smoothed out Axel's discarded sheets of paper, divided each one into four and hung the bits on the wall. Marianne wipes herself with Axel's manuscript and, despite her wretched state, can't help smiling.

Marianne walks stiffly back to her sickbed. In the room across from hers she can see a woman in her twenties, confined to her bed. She knows that Axel has visited her several times during his writing breaks. Like the young woman in Copenhagen, this Greek woman had also been on her honeymoon when an automobile accident left her paralyzed from the neck down. Marianne thinks about fate ruthlessly dealing its cards and is thankful that she's made it this far in one piece.

————

Marianne was worn out after the operation. To perk themselves up, she and Axel bought tickets to an American western at the local cinema. Marianne tottered along, her stomach heavily bandaged. Wearing their fur and duffel coats they settled in at the chilly theatre and opened a bag of roasted sunflower seeds while music filled the room and the film began to glide across the screen. Slowly, the bullet-ridden cowboys, lying heaped on top of one another like so many dead fish, woke up, mounted their horses and rode away, backwards. Axel and Marianne looked at each other in surprise. In the machine room, the projectionist struggled to get the reel the right way round so the audience could watch the film play forward, from the beginning.

LUXURY IN ATHENS

In the middle of December they arrived at long last in Athens. Their friends Per and Else Berit had moved there the year before, and Marianne and Axel collapsed, just about exhausted, in their luxury apartment in Patriarch Ioakim Street. The elevator carried Marianne and Axel directly from the garage to the living room, and for a couple of weeks they enjoyed the longed-for comforts of civilization. Per and Else Berit were delighted to have guests. It was decided that Marianne and Axel would stay over until the new year. The four friends celebrated Christmas Eve in Athens with pork ribs, sauerkraut and all the trimmings — Christmas food sent from Oslo.

In Athens they received a letter, poste restante, from Henrik Groth, Axel's publisher in Oslo. Groth thanked Axel for his letter and wrote that Marianne's appendix had for quite a while preoccupied them more than Eisenhower's stroke: "We didn't even know if Marianne had been handed over to a Macedonian horse castrator or an Albanian sausage-maker (sorry!). Until we knew more it was frightfully unpleasant."[13]

Axel wanted to rent a house so he could get down to work on the new book that crowded his head. Per and Else Berit had heard that the island of Hydra, just three hours from Athens, was an inexpensive and interesting place to settle down. But first Marianne and Axel wanted to see Delphi. Heading for Apollo's realm, they bumped along muddy roads to get nearer to the old gods and perhaps hear the oracle itself.

According to Greek mythology, Zeus dispatched an eagle from points furthest east and furthest west and the place where the birds met was Delphi. In this way spectacular Delphi became the navel of the world. Apollo, the god of Delphi, was a great singer and lyre-player and he led the nine muses who inspired the arts. The oracle of Delphi was unfailingly correct, and men — but no women — flocked to the site with their personal questions.[14] Of those who consulted the oracle, the most famous was King Oedipus, who would come to murder his father and marry his own mother. Axel was fascinated by this myth.

A few days after leaving Athens they parked the blue Beetle at the centre of the world. They got out of the car on the high plateau and looked out over the enormous amphitheatre and the deep valley that was its breathtaking backdrop. There were no signs and no one to collect entry tickets to the historic site. Axel searched for the famous oracle, which turned out to be a rock rather than the hole or fissure in the ground that Marianne had expected. It was her first experience of an ancient Greek theatre. She descended the steps and stood at the bottom, looking up at Axel, at the top, and whispered, "I love you." The sound carried all the way up to him. During a performance, one could hear a pin land on the stage.

Axel fetched his toilet bag from the car and shaved his head. He bayed at the moon like a wolf before meditating and praying to the gods. Marianne regarded him while he sat in the lotus position in a crevice in the side of the mountain, a thin young man in a duffel coat, completely bald. She took out the camera and photographed her peculiar, impulsive lover as he sat there with a smile on his lips.

It was January and the temperature was sinking. The car was uncomfortable as a place to spend the nights. They grew cold when they slept, and making love among the suitcases and seatbacks was awkward.

They headed southward to the Peloponnese and wound up in the dusty little town of Ermioni, where they lodged with an old lady who rented out rooms. From there they could almost see Hydra, a little further north in the Aegean Sea. The woman let them park the Volkswagen in her overgrown garden, while Marianne and Axel scooped up their luggage, typewriter and books and took the first boat.

On board they met a big bear of a man by the name of Papadopoulos, who turned out to be a candy multimillionaire. Papadopoulos had founded the Papa's Sweets factory in California and was eager to speak English. Axel and Marianne pumped him for information. Papadopoulos confirmed what they'd heard in Athens: "There are hundreds of islands in this sea and if you haven't already decided where you're going, you'll never manage to choose one. So get off at the first stop. Hydra is the most beautiful island in the Aegean."

And so it was decided.

Chapter 3

HYDRA

It's raining and cold, in the middle of January. The boat drops anchor far out in the bay. Along with the other passengers, Marianne and Axel are transported to land in small boats. The harbour is shaped like a horseshoe in which fishing boats painted blue and white are moored side by side, bobbing in the water. Small yellow oil-lamps glow in the windows of the whitewashed stone houses that climb up the hillsides from the waterfront. Marianne and Axel walk toward a cluster of lit-up buildings, looking out for a place to spend the night. A few Greeks hasten miserably homeward through the cold rain.

After getting themselves a single room at the Hotel Sophia, they find a café that's open and sit down. Three fluorescent tubes are suspended by wires from the ceiling. Outside the wind blows bitterly. Standing in the middle of the room is a scorching hot oven that looks like an old oil drum, with a pipe that goes straight up and then bends to exit out the window over the entrance. The oven vibrates with heat. A group of Greek men play backgammon and drink ouzo.

One of the younger men is named Jimmy. He can speak some English. He strides over to Marianne and Axel and says, "Hello. Where are you from?" and "I know other English." Marianne and Axel waste no time in arranging to meet Jimmy again the next day so he can direct them to the other English-speaking people on Hydra.

. Two small kittens mewl and beg for food among the tables. A man kicks one of the cats, sending it flying into the wall. Marianne jumps up and cuddles the skinny creature in her lap. Looking at her with incredulity, the local men gesticulate for her benefit — the kitten has fleas. The warning notwithstanding, Marianne and Axel depart the café each bearing a scruffy kitten. They settle into the whitewashed room on the second floor of the Hotel Sophia. Their toes cold in spite of their long underwear and sweaters, they slide into bed. They fall asleep lying close together in the little room, which has a balcony and view of the port, where the boats creak against one another in the waves.

The next day Marianne goes to the pharmacy and buys pipettes with which to feed the kittens milk. But they can't keep the food down. Their eyes big and round, the cats hiss and miaow for food. Together she and Axel decide to end their suffering. Down by the water, Axel knocks the mewing kittens on the head with a stone and throws them in the water. Greedy seabirds swoop down and grapple for the little cats.

Later that day Jimmy shows up as agreed and escorts them to George and Charmian Johnston. Axel and Marianne aren't met with an effusive reception, just a short "Welcome — we're working, but we can meet you at Katsikas'." Katsikas' turns out to be a shop on the corner. The back room serves as a store-room and a café, furnished with four simple wooden tables and some uncomfortable chairs with woven seats. Barrels of strong retsina are stacked against the wall, nearly reaching the ceiling. Octopuses and sheep testicles hang to dry. In the shop at the front the ceiling bristles with suspended baskets, brooms, cooking pans and other essential household utensils. The walls are jammed with foods and tools of various descriptions, and on top of a heap of flour sacks a little cat sits cleaning its front paws.

The Australians George and Charmian Johnston were among

the first foreigners to settle on Hydra. A tall lean man, George used to be a reporter for *Life* magazine and now writes detective novels set in exotic locations under the pseudonym Shane Martin. Shane and Martin are the names of the couple's oldest children. Their third child, Jason, was born on the island. Charmian also makes a living as a writer. She is dark and intense and quarrels frequently with her spouse. The Australian writer-couple helps the new Norwegian arrivals, putting them in contact with the island's only real estate agent and giving them down-to-earth advice about starting life on Hydra.

The island is inhabited by over two thousand Greeks and six expatriates. Besides Axel and Marianne and their guardian angels George and Charmian, the foreign contingent includes Nancy and Patrick Greer. He is Irish and a writer and has settled on Hydra to write. The little group begins to meet regularly, when the mail arrives around noontime and again in the evenings when the day's work is done. Slowly Marianne and Axel are incorporated into the little circle of friends.

———

During those early days on Hydra, Marianne and Axel rented a tiny cheap house. The toilet — a hole in the floor and a bucket of water to flush it with — was in the cellar. They installed themselves with their few belongings and took the boat back to the mainland and the overgrown garden where the Volkswagen was parked. The old landlady peeked with astonishment as they ransacked the car of its furnishings, dragging the back seat and the two front seats to the boat. When they arrived back at Hydra, they carried everything on their heads up to the house. Thus they acquired a sofa and chairs. Now they lacked only a table.

At the local café they had become acquainted with a well-off Albanian named Mimi Laozi. The population of Hydra was predominantly of Albanian, rather than Greek, origin. In the middle of the fifteenth century Albanian refugees came across from the Peloponnese and settled on Hydra. Mainly poor shepherds and farmers, they put down roots on the island and in the 1950s many Hydriots still spoke Albanian.

Mimi had grown up in the Hydra Hotel, near the big pharmacy, and her cellar was full of old things that had been stored there for decades. Invited to poke around in the cellar to see if there was anything they could use, Marianne and Axel found two old taverna chairs and a wooden cable spool. The spool, which had washed up during a winter storm, could serve as a coffee table. They thanked Mimi and laboriously rolled the spool along the paving stones, satisfied with the day's catch.

The seats from the car, the coffee table of weathered grey wood and the bed and spring mattress were what they had in the beginning. They eventually acquired some straight-backed Greek chairs with woven seats and carved wooden backs. There was electricity for just an hour in the morning and an hour in the evening. They burned kerosene lamps; water came from the communal wells at the top of the road.

Axel wore out his fingertips writing. Marianne enjoyed the place and took pleasure in feeling the smooth-worn stones under her feet. She made vegetable stews on the kerosene stove and attuned her daily rhythm in time with Axel's. Meat was a luxury; they ate mostly vegetables and lentils. She made stock from olive oil and herbs, and cooked with coal. The retsina tasted like cough medicine, but it was cheap and they soon grew accustomed to it. Retsina, which derived its special flavour from pine resin, had been produced in Greece for over three thousand years. Marianne and Axel bought three-litre wicker-wrapped jugs with handles, trading in the empties for full bottles at the shop. They ate feta cheese fished from barrels of brine. They adopted a pair of stray dogs and fed the scrawny cats that sniffed hopefully around the house. They were blessed with sun, a zeal for work and each other.

Marianne felt free.

The port of Hydra is flanked by white houses that ascend the hills like seats in an amphitheatre, with the waterfront as the orchestra pit. Towering 590 metres above the sea is Mount Ere, the highest point on the island. Just below the mountaintop gleams the whitewashed monastery dedicated to the Prophet Elias.

Socializing took place down in the arc of the waterfront, then as now. Katsikas' and a few other coffeehouses were concentrated around the statue of the island's great hero, Captain Koundouriotis. One of the most illustrious men in Greek history, Pavlos Koundouriotis led the Navy to important victories against the Turkish fleet during the Balkan Wars and was later elected the first president of Greece. Turned to stone, he gazed out to sea, his back to the cafés where coffee and retsina were served. In one of the streets behind Koundouriotis lay the post office. Other than that the harbour had the character of a boatyard. The workshops stood cheek by jowl and steady hammering could be heard at the café tables.

Once a base for the Greek Navy, Hydra was proud of its tradition of ship-building. Many distinguished captains came from the island. Their fleets had fought for Greece in several wars and had formed the foundation for Hydra's prosperity in the eighteenth and nineteenth centuries. In the 1950s the island's former ship-owning and naval families still resided in their old mansions on the hillsides. Many of these estates later passed into the hands of foreigners; some were turned into museums.

Most days Marianne saw little of the womenfolk. Passing doors that were ajar, she caught glimpses of mothers and daughters, in aprons and shoes with worn-down heels, as they scrubbed the floors on their hands and knees. Or she passed them as they stood outside their houses, whitewashing the walls with their long-handled brushes.

Every Sunday after dinner the women emerged in their grandest finery. In high-heels and dresses fitted snugly at the waist and bust, they drank pastis and ate ice cream and cakes, accompanied by their husbands and their smartly turned out children. Perhaps there had been a child's christening or another occasion that made them open the doors to the second floors in their homes. Seldom used, these formal drawing rooms were furnished with large bureaus topped by crocheted doilies, the drawers filled with the family's finest bed linens, tablecloths and silverware. In the event of a baptism, wedding or funeral, the doors to the fancy parlour could be opened and the shutters pushed aside to allow the sunlight to pour in over the best furniture in the house.

A death was marked by a great procession of mourners through the streets. If a woman died without having attained the status of wife and mother, her body was clad in bridal regalia. Instead of marrying the man her parents had chosen for her, she was married in the afterlife. Candles were lit around the coffin. Flowers, handkerchiefs and money were laid upon the deceased, who was embraced and kissed on the forehead.[15]

When a person had taken his own life, however, the mourners bore a closed coffin and kept to the back lanes, their eyes cast down in shame. Some years later Marianne would witness the mourners of Mimi Laozi, who had given them their first pieces of furniture, as they walked with heavy steps along the back streets.

An older man named Jimmy always took up a position at the end of the procession. Whenever there was a funeral, he followed the mourners through the streets. He walked with a rolling gait, a little splay-footed, and always dressed neatly in a dark suit and a flat cap. Jimmy made his living by selling the deceased's possessions that were donated to him by the family. After the funeral, when the clothing and other effects had been sorted, Jimmy came down to the port to peddle the wares in his straw basket. "Do you need shoes today? Very good shoes!"

Jimmy was one of the few Greeks who spoke a little English. He had gone to the United States after the war and had saved what he made peeling potatoes and washing dishes at a Greek restaurant. Returning to Hydra with his earnings, he went through all his money wining and dining his friends. Jimmy had been a poor man ever since.

BUYING A HOUSE

Marianne observed Greek daily life through her Norwegian eyes. It was like going back to another time. The foreigners who were there had made their way to Hydra in protest against the brassy commercialism of the modern world. Axel found the tranquility he needed to write, and when they were both certain that Hydra was the place they wanted to be, they decided to buy their own house.

Axel had received an advance of forty thousand kroner — about six thousand U.S. dollars — from his publisher, and now they could afford to buy a little whitewashed haven for themselves. For about two and a half thousand dollars they found a house like an eagle's nest, cemented into the steep contour of the mountainside, with a view over the houses below and the sea beyond. The house was in need of repairs. They drew up the figures in a notebook:

House: 14,840
Floor: 2,400
Bricklayer: 6,000
Electricity: 2,000
Bathroom: 800
Total: 26,050 kroner

When all the expenses were paid they had just over two thousand dollars to tide them over until Axel's next book was published.

With their own address and a view of the blue sea, Marianne and Axel felt like royalty. The house consisted of a kitchen and a spacious living room on the first floor. They bought big straw mats to hang on the walls, which made it more cozy. A narrow set of open stairs went up to the second level, which was a single room. Francisco, the carpenter, made a worktable and Axel ensconced himself there on the upper floor, with his typewriter and his books.

The house lay on Kala Pigadia Street, on the way to the large wells that in the old days had supplied the whole of Hydra with water. In the cool shadows of the large trees that surrounded the twin wells, folks gathered to exchange news and stories. It was an advantage to live near the wells on this otherwise dry and barren island, so the neighbourhood along Kala Pigadia was among the more affluent. The mayor lived a stone's throw below Marianne and Axel.

Kala Pigadia was transformed into a riverbed when it rained. High stone ledges flanking the street kept the water from rushing into the houses and served as sidewalks when it flooded, as it did now during the winter. The widest thoroughfares were constructed so two donkeys loaded with side-baskets could pass one another. The less trafficked lanes were wide enough for only one donkey at a time. In some places Marianne could stretch out her arms and touch the houses on either side. Outside the entrances to the houses sat old men with canes and their diminutive wives dressed in black.

"*Kalimera sas.*" Good morning to you.

"*Yassas.*" Hello.

The streets were redolent of donkey shit, which people gathered up to fertilize their flowers and trees. With spindly legs and long erect ears, the animals toiled up the roads, bearing planks and schoolbooks, casks of retsina and roof tiles, and everything else that had to be hauled up from the port. The moneyed Hydriots resided high up in the town. The five monasteries on the island were also located high on the mountainside, as close to God as they could get.

Packed closely together in the narrow lanes lay the whitewashed stone houses with their orange roof tiles. When a child grew up and married a new house was built against the old one on the family's property. The new house had a separate entrance and as a rule the doors faced downward toward the port instead of straight toward the street. The buildings evolved in many irregular forms in this way. Struck by this architectural anarchy, Henry Miller rhapsodized over "this wild and naked perfection of Hydra."[16]

Marianne and Axel lived a good life, far from Norway. Marianne missed brown goat cheese and cold milk, but not life in the north. She had very little contact with her people back home. Mother sent letters expressing her uneasiness regarding her daughter, who had left against their wishes; she could scarcely believe that Marianne had a roof over her head. Preferring distance, Marianne didn't reply. Liberation — wasn't that moving to a Greek island and going barefoot, away from the watchful eyes of her parents? Marianne was well aware that for her this wasn't just a quest for adventure, but also an escape from Oslo.

Marianne had never before seen anything so beautiful. The island enchanted her, and she felt at home. At the same time she felt that she stood out and was noticed — that she was *someone*. It was almost as if her girlish daydreams had come true. Her body brown and her hair sunbleached, she walked shoeless on the smooth stones. This was freedom. This was how she wanted it.

———

There was little work to be found on the island and very little money in circulation. When Marianne and Axel first came, Hydra's women were clad in black. The local men pushed off at dawn to fish, long before the children went to school and the town awakened. In the morning the port was the commercial centre where the boats were unloaded, fish and vegetables were sold and donkeys hired for transport.

Very little grew in the barren landscape. People were dependent on the fish they hauled out of the sea and the imported vegetables they purchased. Piped water had not yet come to the island and the soil wasn't cultivated. There was just stone, stone, stone. Rainwater and kerosene lamps.

The Greek community was so small that it took just a few months to establish a nodding acquaintance with almost every family. The expatriates didn't mix much with the Greeks but knew of deaths and births. Everyone knew everyone else's business.

The foreign residents who had no income on Hydra were dependent on the cheques that arrived in the post. The ferry bringing mail pulled into the harbour at 11:30, drawing the expatriates to the port. After the letters and parcels had been sorted, they dashed to the post office — had a short story or a poem brought in some money? It was a ritual: first the post office and then shopping for food. After that, a glass of retsina. The wine made it easier to climb the steps of the steep hill homeward, heavy basket in hand.

Putting up their house as security, Marianne and Axel had a one-year line of credit at Katsikas'. Sophia and Antony were a kindly couple who ran the shop. They took new expatriates under their wings, helping with the practicalities of life on the island and extending credit to those whose cheques came at long intervals. It was a relationship of mutual benefit and respect. The foreigners who lived there didn't see themselves as tourists and didn't dress in miniskirts or saunter around the port in bikinis.

Nonetheless, Hydra was seen as a kind of free state where people could do what they wanted, living out their desires without much interference. The foreign community grew steadily. The island had also long been favoured by rich Athenians who came on weekends and holidays. They had their little palaces high on the hillsides, with magnificent views over the Aegean, and they arrived for the weekends with their kitchen maids and other servants and baskets full of fresh flowers.

Marianne observed and breathed in the atmosphere of Greek daily life. They were foreigners — xenoi — and the island's inhabitants regarded them with friendly curiosity. The Greeks with whom they developed real friendships came from aristocratic and intellectual circles. That very first summer they got to know George Lialios. An educated young man, George spoke several languages and was interested in philosophy. Aside from serving in the diplomatic corps, his father was a composer and musician. George introduced Marianne and Axel to many of the highly educated and wealthy Greeks who lived or vacationed on the island. The Lialios family had a large estate on the Peloponnese where they produced olive oil and had also invested in a stately house with a view over the whole town of Hydra.

Inviting them to drink wine before the big open fireplace in his kitchen, George presented Marianne and Axel to a core of Greek intellectuals who had come to Hydra for many of the same reasons as they had. They were young people with various artistic ambitions who were searching for something. They were also introduced to the Russian Lily Mack, who was married to Christian Heidsieck from the famous champagne dynasty. Lily was so wild and eccentric that Marianne was almost afraid of her, but Christian was a potter and he taught Marianne to work with clay. When the ceramic objects were baking in the oven Christian and Marianne sat in the ochre-painted restaurant near his house in Kamini and they read Ibsen together. Christian's English was fluent, while Marianne slowly broadened her vocabulary through Shakespeare and translations of Ibsen.

COCKTAILS WITH THE UPPER CRUST

In spite of their poor dress and simple standard of living, Marianne and Axel found themselves being invited to drinks and cocktail parties by the Greek upper class. The Greeks were awed that the young blond couple had come all the way to Hydra and were curious about them. Rich Madame Paouri — who painted the window frames of all her houses a special shade of blue and who had donated blue dresses with white dots to all the schoolgirls on Hydra — held the swankiest parties.

"Drinks before dinner. Six o'clock at our house."

Marianne and Axel went in t-shirts and trousers, which was just about all the clothing they had. It was at one of these cocktail parties that they first met the shipping magnate Aristotle Onassis. When Onassis heard that they were from Norway he said, "Oh, I go fishing there!" He'd spent several seasons salmon fishing in Norway and he asked how they had come to Hydra. Oh, so Axel was an author? What did he write about?

Their presence at posh gatherings was soon taken for granted. Themselves shoeless, they were served by stewards in impeccable white uniforms. On board the yachts champagne poured from spouts shaped like dolphin mouths. Young Greek women married to old rich men with big bellies mingled on the luxurious boats. The women had diamonds on their fingers and dresses that Marianne had seen only in magazines.

———

So far Marianne was satisfied with being the muse who sat at Axel's feet while he created. She read his manuscript and made suggestions. A little red star marked the places where she lost interest in the story but she didn't speak about it until Axel said that he appreciated her notations and asked her to elaborate. She explained where the narrative engaged her and where it ceased to hold her attention, and she told him that in her opinion he sometimes over-expounded, going on for longer than he needed to. Axel listened to what she had to say but became irritated when she spoke of numbers of pages, retorting that a book needed a certain length to be called a book.

Axel was still trying to make Marianne more self-aware and conscious of her own strengths. She filled page after page in her journal with her doodles and poems, thoughts and dreams. Pen and paper in hand, she often went to the pebble beach in Kamini, where she sat on a rock and jotted down her last dream on a blank page in her journal:

> Was about to get married. Choosing an apartment
> with lots of windows. Had a choice between the first
> and third floors. There was a hole in the floor with a
> railing around it. Thought the third was best because
> then no one could throw anything down at me.
> Green curtains, had to shut the windows so the dogs
> wouldn't fall out. The house was in the middle of Oslo.
> Later met a train carrying refugees at Central Station
> and it surprised me that the police didn't come.
>   I wanted a child that I could dress up and wheel
> around the streets in a baby carriage. Wanted just one,
> preferably a boy.

Foreigners came and settled on Hydra in growing numbers. Many of the newcomers were writers and painters. Some months after the arrival of Marianne and Axel, a young Swedish writer named Göran Tunström showed up. At that time having published just one collection of poems, he'd worked as a grave-digger to scrape together enough money to travel south. He'd heard about the Norwegian author Axel Jensen and rented a house just below Marianne and Axel in Kala Pigadia. Just two years older than the likeable Swede, Marianne thought of him as the little neighbour boy who came to visit. She stood on the terrace and called maternally, "Göran, time to come and eat!" Marianne nicknamed him "Bastiano" and made cacao for him in the evenings when the air had a chilly draft.

Axel always wanted to push ideas and myths as far as he could when he discussed them during their evenings out. One person he often ended up arguing with was the Englishman David Goshen. They provoked each other and when their arguments came to a head they nearly wound up brawling. It wasn't unusual for conversations to heat up and temperaments to flare among the foreigners on Hydra. Goshen was married to a Scottish aristocrat who was a sculptor. He wore pyjamas during the day, had titles and a spinet, but no money. The first time Marianne tasted stinging nettle soup it was at the home of David and his wife, who were so poor that they picked wild greens and berries to eke out their subsistence.

———

The days were pleasant. Axel worked diligently on the follow-up to *Ikaros*. Marianne followed her own routine. Shopping at Katsikas', she announced one day that she would like to sell a kilo of rice. The proprietors felt that Marianne's Greek had become good enough that they could correct her, so they taught her how to say that she would like to *buy* a kilo of rice.

For Marianne, that first year on Hydra was wonderful. They had established a home base and a routine of daily tasks for themselves. Meanwhile, Axel was increasingly in demand as an author back in Norway on account of the enormous success of *Ikaros*.

Marianne remained behind on Hydra when Axel was travelling. She had tumbled into the cream of Greek society, and when Axel was on one of his trips to Oslo, she ran into Peter Nomikos at the port. He belonged to one of the prominent shipping families in Greece and was studying engineering in London. When he heard that Marianne was on her own, he invited her on board his yacht, where a professor from his English university was a guest along with his wife. Marianne accepted, though she wasn't feeling very well. She had contracted ringworm from their adopted cats; her face was covered with small black rings just under her skin. Peter immediately decided to dispatch her to his family's doctor in Athens.

The next morning a seaman from the yacht picked her up outside her house. Marianne trotted off in sandals and sailor pants, a little bag under her arm. A suave, gallant man about her own age, Peter told her she was incredibly beautiful, as many other men had. He attended to her every need, and they sailed southward until the sun was high in the sky. The little party anchored in a bay and shared a sumptuous lunch of smoked salmon and lobster before setting course for Piraeus. The Nomikos family home in Athens consisted of an entire apartment block with elevators descending directly into the various residences. Peter had the penthouse. Marianne was offered the best medical help from the family's doctor. With blood-red medicine smeared on every blemish, Marianne looked as if she'd come down with spotted fever when she rode the ferry back to Hydra and Axel, who had returned from Oslo and was waiting for her.

———

It was 1958 and Axel was well into the novel he was writing. They had been on Hydra for nearly a year but as work on the book proceeded the predictability of their lives was rattled by money worries. They lived on advances from the publisher and their finances were a recurring source of conflict. Henrik Groth, Axel's publisher, had tremendous faith in the new book, believing it could be ground-breaking literature of which Norwegian readers had never seen the likes.

Marianne was lonely when Axel went to Norway, just as she had been in Oslo when Axel was travelling and she had feared losing him. Now, together on Hydra, discord arose between them with growing frequency. She felt that Axel wasn't fully present in her life, and Axel was vexed by her insecurity. The expatriates sat at Katsikas' and introduced themselves to newly arrived foreigners: "I'm a writer"; "I'm a painter"; "I write poetry." Thus they presented themselves, one after the other. When it was Marianne's turn, she said with as much conviction as she could muster: "I'm living. Life is my art." She caught Axel's withering look and shrank from it. In Hydra's arty circles, no one ever questioned what she did:

she had always been embraced by the Greeks and the resident foreigners alike. Though no one expected her to take up writing or painting, she couldn't help feeling inferior because she didn't stand on her own feet creatively or economically. The "only" thing that Axel asked of her was that she find her own place in the world and, as he put it, become a complete human being. That was easier said than done. Why did she never feel that she was good enough as she was?

———

Some hundred metres above their house lived an old woman known as Kyria — Mrs. — Sophia. Sophia sold flour and sugar and a few other basic necessities from her house and passersby could sit down there to a light meal. The little room was painted light green, the moulding in the brightest shades of pastel pink. Crosses and icons hung on the walls, along with delightful arrangements of pots and pans, ropes of garlic and family photographs. Marianne regularly stopped in and sat a while with the grey-haired woman. Short and almost as wide as she was tall, Sophia wore a kerchief and apron and had a strong, warm gaze. Noticing when Marianne was sad, she stroked her cheek and comforted her as if she were a little girl.

"*Kardoula mou, s'agapo.*" Sweetheart, I love you.

It was soothing to sit quietly with the old woman. It softened the lump in her chest that formed when she had rowed with Axel or when she feared he would abandon her.

Sophia took care of a pair of orphan siblings as if they were her own. Marianne saw them often when she was visiting Sophia, observing how the old woman cared for them without fuss, as she comforted Marianne when she needed it. The children had never gone to school and were illiterate. The girl was short and skinny and didn't say much. The boy was disabled, and one of his legs dragged. The story was that a donkey had kicked his mother in the stomach when she was pregnant with him. He went fishing whenever he was offered the chance, scuttling bare-legged down the stony lanes to the sea. Marianne heard the other children shout taunts at him as he limped down the street. Marianne thought about how a Greek tragedy was always close at hand.

―――

Axel wrote intensively from morning to evening. When Marianne felt unable to keep up with Axel's rapid transitions of thought and his impulsive actions she retreated to the role she knew she had mastered: housewife. They were like night and day. She was practical and happiest when the days were predictable. He floated in the clouds and lived through his work, eager to break boundaries in literature as well as in life.

Axel wrote regularly to John Starr Cooke on the other side of the Atlantic. The two of them exchanged long, somewhat incoherent letters with each other about how everything on the planet was connected. On the 16th of September, 1958, John wrote that he had become a damn good astrologer and asked Axel to send him the date, time and place of his birth — and Marianne's — so he could cast their horoscopes.[17]

Axel dabbled in astrology and had filled a pad with drawings, astrological charts and interpretations of the various star signs. Born under the air sign of Aquarius, Axel noted that people born under this sign sought new ways to express old ideas; for Aquarians the path was more important than the end point. Marianne was a Taurus, an earth sign, and Axel had written with a thin black marker in his notepad that Taureans were preoccupied with family, single-minded, stubborn and didn't find it easy to accept others' points of view, but they were often kind. With Venus guiding inspiration and intuition for Taureans, he wrote, they love beauty and harmony.

On one of his trips to Oslo, Axel crossed paths with a beautiful dark-haired woman. He invited her to Hydra, convinced that they were meant for each other and that this woman aroused something different in him than did Marianne. He spent five days together with this woman and was in love when he came back to Hydra. Marianne stood in the kitchen and heard him say, gravely, "I've found another woman, she's dark-haired and she's coming." Axel had made up his mind that his relationship with Marianne was over.

Her grandmother had told Marianne that as long as she was breathing she was still alive, and she must always remember that. Marianne remembered Momo picking her up when she'd fallen off her bicycle as a little girl. "*BREATHE*, Marianne, *BREATHE*," she'd exhorted her, and the pain had abated. Thinking about Axel, Marianne slowly inhaled and exhaled to keep calm.

She inspected herself in the mirror and contemplated her sunbleached hair. She decided then to try to become someone else, to become the one that Axel would want. She put on tennis shoes, slung her bag on her arm and took the boat to Piraeus. She went into the first hair salon she came across and asked to have her hair dyed black.

The next morning, back on Hydra, she looked with surprise at the dark hair on the pillow and asked herself who she was and what she was going to do with her life. She was terrified of going home and admitting defeat. Were Mother and Father right after all when they said that Axel wasn't someone to count on? Marianne packed her bag and decided to go to Athens for a few days — in any case she couldn't be home on Hydra when the other woman came. She took the next boat and checked into a fleabag hotel in the old part of the city called Plaka.

———

In Athens Per and Else Berit learned the latest news from Hydra and on the 8th of September, 1958, Else Berit wrote a letter to their common friends in Oslo telling them that her old prediction had been realized. The break-up between Marianne and Axel was now a fact:

Axel is a strange person, with an impressive intellect on the one hand and a vulnerable, sensitive, CHILDISH mind on the other. Marianne, who can't follow all of his bizarre, high-flying thoughts, tries to assert herself in other ways, by striking at Axel's weaknesses, wounding him and so on. It's impossible for this kind of relationship to be harmonious and before Axel went to Norway both of them were aware that they had reached a critical point in their lives together.

When Axel was in Norway he met (as you know) a woman with whom, after 5 days of acquaintance, he became deeply fascinated, so much so that after he returned to Greece he couldn't forget her. He claimed that in her he found something he had not found in any other woman, and that he could not continue his life with Marianne before he had arrived at an understanding with this other woman. The end of it was that he and Marianne agreed to separate, and the other woman, Sonja, is coming to Greece to live with Axel on Hydra. He has sent her train tickets and pocket money and is just waiting to hear when she's coming.

Marianne is staying in Athens and wants to try to get a job here, somewhere or other, because understandably enough she has no desire to go home. She was amazingly calm and realized the inevitability of Axel's action but it is of course very hard for her to know that someone else is going to take her place in the house she and Axel fixed up and made a home of, caring for the cat and dog, etc. etc. She says that she has never felt as close to Axel as now.[18]

In big bold letters Else Berit related how she'd advised Marianne not to run right back to Axel should Sonja fail to arrive or if Axel discovered that he'd made a mistake. She maintained that Marianne should think profoundly about what being together with Axel would really mean over the course of a whole life. True enough, Marianne had matured considerably during the last eight months she had spent on Hydra, in the company of all kinds of odd artistic types. She had become broad-minded and open, but Else Berit believed that deep inside she was too conventional to spend the rest of her life living like a Bohemian, something she would be condemned to do with Axel. Marianne would probably be a good deal happier with a less complicated man who would give her a more orthodox relationship, and Else Berit hoped for the sake of all parties that Marianne and Axel wouldn't bolt into each other's arms in desperation if Sonja didn't show up.

From California, John sent Axel a letter studded with "dear friend!" and exclamation points. John thought it was bad news that good Marianne was now out of Axel's life. He had felt that Axel had been in safe waters with Marianne around him. Now he was less certain about how things would go for Axel — he had to sit down with Axel's horoscope to see what direction this would take.[19]

———

The first night in Athens, Marianne lay in grey mouldy-smelling sheets, reading a Kafka paperback and crying herself to sleep. She was awakened the next day by morning light streaming through the window. She put on her big sunglasses and decided to start the day at the legendary Café Zonar's, just behind Syntagma Square.

Zonar's was a big posh café with orange awnings and cobalt-blue cushions on the chairs, and waiters in white shirts, black trousers and long black aprons. It was a regular meeting place for writers and intellectuals, a kind of Greek version of the Theatre Café home in Oslo. Inside, patrons dined on gourmet food at tables draped in white damask, while the café outside served the most delicious Greek cakes. Marianne sank wearily onto a chair and ordered an ouzo. Lost in thought, she suddenly heard a car jamming on the brakes and someone shouting:

"Marianne! Thank God you're here! You're my guardian angel!"

The voice belonged to Eileen, an Englishwoman married to Sam Barclay, one of the heirs to Barclays Bank in England. Barclay had a huge yacht that he had built himself and used to take tourists and wealthy people on cruises. Marianne knew Sam from Hydra, where he'd helped her and Axel hire workers when they fixed up the house with funds from *Ikaros*.

Plumping down into a chair at Marianne's table in her wide-brimmed straw hat, Eileen chattered about her fantastic new lover. She implored Marianne to get her out of a jam by taking her place as cook and hostess on the yacht so Eileen could avoid joining her husband on the next trip. During the winter, when they weren't sailing, the couple lived on the island of Spetses. Barclay's wife was tired of life in a primitive Greek house in the winter and drifting on the waves like a vagabond in the summer.

For Marianne, homeless and abandoned, the offer was like a gift from the gods.

———

At 8:30 the following morning she shows up at the harbour in Piraeus. Sam is standing on the deck of his schooner when she arrives, and Marianne hears a boy's thin voice asking, "Isn't Mama coming?" Sam answers, "No, your mother isn't coming, but Marianne will take care of us." Wearing high heels and a slim skirt, Marianne boards the *Stormie Seas*, glad for the opportunity to cast aside her land-bound drama for six weeks. Work on board the boat allows her to stay in Greece for a while longer, even though another woman is coming to take her place in the house on Hydra.

Off on her own journey and no longer at the mercy of his whims, she felt free of Axel. She could cook and she would easily manage to look after Sam's son. The tempetuous emotional side of life had let her down but never the practical side. If she was paid to work on a boat on the open sea, then it was just a matter of taking responsibility and proving herself worthy of the job.

Sam sailed to small idyllic islands and along the Turkish coast. Marianne cooked for an older man and his young wife who had rented the boat and crew for a month and a half. Apart from Sam, the crew comprised a young Greek sailor who knew the local waters and Marianne, newly dark-haired. She read fairy tales to seven-year-old James and carried out her other simple duties on board.

Anchoring in the ocean-filled Santorini caldera, they were invited to a traditional three-day-long Greek wedding along with several hundred guests. Sam, who spoke fluent Greek, immediately accepted the generous invitation. The priest sang and intoned while people crossed themselves and kissed the Bible and various icons. There were bridesmaids and groomsmen and the small church was full to the rafters. After the ceremony, the dancing and music continued until dawn, when the little band of travellers staggered back to the boat for a few hours sleep.

The next day they decided to visit the volcano crater, which rose above the water in the centre of the caldera. Marianne wore an Egyptian scarab Axel had given her on a thin leather thong around her neck. She decided to sacrifice the scarab and rid herself of everything that bound her to Axel. Marianne had tried to suppress her grief over Axel when she joined Sam on board the boat. Now she just wanted to sail away from it all, keeping her feelings bottled up.

White churches the size of dollhouses glowed serenely against the dark lava along the way up the slope of the volcano. Marianne lit the wicks that floated on saucers filled with olive oil and came to a stop where many before her had mumbled their prayers. At the top, she hurled the scarab with all her might out into the crater before turning and going back to the boat.

———

Both Sam and Marianne had been betrayed and rejected. Sam was a handsome man, slim and tall with light hair and a body bronzed by the sun. And Marianne was free. She was heartsick but was free to love on a beautiful sailboat that took her away from all the sadness on Hydra, and together they lifted each other out of a difficult time.

Along the side of the schooner hung baskets of live lobsters. There were big English brunches and late dinners in small whitewashed towns. The stars above gave the endless Greek night sky a pale glow. The sky was three-dimensional: beyond the stars there were other stars, and beyond these yet more stars. They sailed along the coast of Turkey, heard wolves howling under the full moon and wandered among the colonnades of ancient temples in the company of lumbering tortoises.

The couple Marianne looked after on board the boat gave her a cookbook when she signed off after six weeks of sailing. Inside the book, entitled *Can the Greek Cook?*, their inscription read, "The Norwegians can. Marianne has proved."

Marianne's encounter with Sam was fleeting and without strings. The interlude allowed her to muster the strength she needed to return to Oslo and admit defeat. Now she could go home and say, "Alright, you were right. It's not Axel I'm going to marry."

Chapter 4

NEW MARIANNE

Marianne disembarked in Piraeus and went straight home to Per and Else Berit, with whom she'd left her things. The last time Marianne and Axel had been there together, Per and Else Berit had become so fed up with the incessant arguing that they'd thrown them out.

Now they told Marianne that they thought the boat trip had changed her. Else Berit wrote in a letter that the woman who had come back was a "COMPLETELY NEW Marianne." She was more serene and self-confident and she had a clear and mature view of her relationship with Axel. In short, she'd grown up. The couple in Athens were astonished at the extent of the transformation. Marianne claimed to love Axel more than ever before — it was only now that she understood how much she cared for him. She was nonetheless prepared to live without him and to find herself a good job.

When Axel visited Athens to take care of some financial matters it was inevitable that he and Marianne would meet. Axel had been on a six-week drinking binge. The dark-haired woman he'd met in Oslo had sold the ticket and pocketed the money. Else Berit wrote to friends that it was amusing to witness the sangfroid with which Marianne handled Axel and how this threw him off balance. He fell in love with her all over again.

As Marianne dried herself after a shower, Axel watched her

from the bathroom doorway. He walked into the room, looked at Marianne, who stood in the middle of the floor with a towel wrapped around her, and said, "Will you marry me, Marianne?"

Marianne's stint on the yacht had extinguished her fear. She felt self-possessed: she had accomplished something on her own and had learned that she could stand on her own feet, without Axel. And yet she had been waiting her whole life to receive such a proposal and be carried off by her lover, as had happened in Momo's stories. Marianne agreed to become Mrs. Jensen.

Else Berit said that when someone like Axel went as far as proposing marriage something powerful must lie behind it, so she could understand that Marianne had accepted. The two of them could find happiness only if they began on an entirely new footing, wrote Else Berit in a letter to Norway, adding, "I believe in a marriage between them as long as the new order lasts."[20]

———

On the 22nd of October, 1958, Marianne and Axel were married by Father Duncan in the Anglican church in Athens, with Per and Else Berit as best man and matron of honour. Twenty-three-year-old Marianne was dressed in a white silk blouse that her girlfriend Unni had been sent by her family in America. It had buttons up the back and a band of gold ribbon at the neck. Over the blouse she wore a dark blue suit her mother had sewn; the jacket had raglan sleeves and a single button at the throat and the pencil skirt was slit up the back. Having borrowed gloves from Else Berit, Marianne could now be married — in keeping with English custom — in something old, something new, something borrowed and something blue.

The church was being renovated; five or six stone masons sat on scaffolding below the ceiling, dangling their legs. Marianne and Axel kissed each other every time the priest turned to pray to the Heavenly Father. When Marianne was about to get up after kneeling, her narrow skirt slid up her thighs and stayed there. The workmen, who had been asked to remain quiet during the ceremony, couldn't hold back their laughter. Too embarrassed to yank down her skirt in front of the priest, Marianne just stood there, blushing. From above came the sound of suppressed sniggers.

The gravity of the situation caused Axel's English to falter when the time came to repeat the marriage vows. Father Duncan looked at Axel and prompted:

"I give you my troth . . ."

Axel repeated:

"I give you my throat . . ."

After the church there was champagne at home with Per and Else Berit, while letters and telegrams were read out. The greetings that had been pouring through the mail slot for days had been saved for the big day. Bouquets of flowers decorated the living room and there was a festive air in the apartment.

Marianne came from a well-furnished home on the West Side of Oslo and a proper married couple needed tableware, regardless of the Bohemian nature of the wedding. Two potato dishes, two large serving platters, a sauce boat and silver-plated fish cutlery for eight had been sent from Oslo to Greece. But the wedding gifts from Marianne's mother weren't easy to claim. Marianne couldn't afford to pay the duties and she didn't have the money to send the package back to Norway either, so it all ended up waiting at customs in Athens for ages.

The wedding dinner was celebrated at a luxury hotel at Astir Beach, outside Athens. Per and Else Berit had married there six months earlier, with Marianne and Axel as best man and maid of honour. That had been such a success that they decided to have another party at the same place. The four old friends played leapfrog and horsed around on the beach before dinner was served by liveried waiters with freshly ironed cloth napkins over their arms. The meal was followed by quite a few glasses of Courvoisier. Per and Else Berit had fun scaring Axel with the prospect of a fifteen-minute bridal waltz, like the one they'd endured themselves. Axel was quiet and pale with anxiety. But the dance turned out to be a very comfortable foxtrot and, besides, the newlyweds were not the only people on the dance floor. Per and Else Berit felt short-changed.

Marianne and Axel stayed with Per and Else Berit for four days after the wedding and their married life began blissfully. Sucking on his pipe with a proprietary air, Axel was evidently proud to possess a wife. Marianne, who could finally call herself Mrs. Jensen, was euphoric.

———

It was the start of a good period. Axel surprised Marianne with the improvements he had made to their house on Hydra. Its whitewashed walls glistening, the eagle's nest in Kala Pigadia was almost unrecognizable to Marianne. Realizing how much it would mean to her, he'd rolled up his sleeves and set to work during her absence. She wept with joy as she took in everything that Axel had done.

Axel threw himself back into his writing, while Marianne sketched and noted her thoughts and dreams between the blue marbled covers of her diary.

14/12-58
Sunday with sun and wonderful warmth, and I'm sitting here scribbling and soaking it up. It's pure summer here, just ten days until Christmas Eve. It's incredible.

Axel was angry with me yesterday. Because of the book Line, the numbers of pages etc. I never learn. God knows how many times this same thing has happened. Hope it doesn't happen again. I will try, try. But if I blurt it out, ok, it gets blurted out. There's nothing that can be done about that. But

why does Axel get so worked up every single time?
Well, we'll figure it out sooner or later. The first
little disagreement (quarrel) since we were married
1 month and 20 days ago. Well, I'd better be off to
the post office and treat myself to an orangeade. It's
Sunday and the weather is like summer.

15/12-58
Slept til 11:30 and ran to town, but the boat hadn't
come, engine troubles at Poros. Charmian, George
et al. "celebrating" and a chair appeared under your
bottom and a glass of retsina was pressed into your
hand before you'd said hi. Cheers and how are you.
I wasn't really in the mood for it, but came around
eventually. Magda was unhappy and feeling very low,
and Charmian tried to talk her out of it.
    We ended up eating lunch out, the whole bunch of
us, and I brought some things from the bakery home
to Axel. Slept after cleaning up but feel fine amidst all
the animals on the sofa with my diary in my lap. Now
I'm going to read Pasternak . . .
    Nearly gale winds today.

16/12-58
Dismal in town today. No one said anything. The
boat came late so there won't be any post until this
afternoon. Just a little fishing boat as far as the eye
could see. I'm enjoying myself here on my rock and
when I close my eyes and hear the sea I'm suddenly
in Larkollen. I'm not really homesick but can't help
thinking of Larkollen now and then.
    Here I am on Hydra in Greece, with the ocean all
around, married, with a house, garden, terrace, dogs
and a key around my neck — it's almost impossible to

believe. It's true: nothing ventured, nothing gained. It's better to try than to sit on your rear end and say, "no, it's never going to work." There will always come a day, sooner or later, when one regrets it and says, "why the hell didn't I try?"

It's windy and drizzling and my backside is freezing, enough for now.

———

While Axel was in the throes of a particularly intense period of writing, Marianne visited Per and Else Berit in Athens for a change of pace. She took along Sam's son, seven-year-old James, whom she'd befriended during her weeks on board the *Stormie Seas*. Little James came with a hot forehead and shiny eyes and had to be put straight to bed, where he lay for a week with a fever that spiked up to 40 degrees Celsius.

To make the most of having female company, Else Berit took off as much time from the office as she could manage. A week later, Axel rang the doorbell unexpectedly, to everyone's pleasant surprise. He had been working day and night revising his manuscript and needed a break. Axel took over the dinner preparations, bowling everyone over with an Indian curry that he served with champagne while donning a turban festooned with the ladies' jewellery. Else Berit thought that Marianne had become kinder and considerably more mature, and Marianne herself felt that she'd marshalled her inner strength during her time on the yacht with Sam. Axel, who used to give free reign to his dominating personality, without making concessions to his working hosts or their wooden floor, had become quieter and more considerate. Marianne believed that this would last, and she believed in Axel and his promise of faithfulness.

LINE

That spring Marianne and Axel took jobs together on Sam's schooner. They needed the money and Sam needed help on the cruise, which would carry a group of English students around Greek waters. Axel had delivered the first draft of his novel to Cappelen. A sailor at heart, he was happy when he was on the water. The newlyweds had thrashed things out and life had become serene. Sam knew Marianne's story, as she knew his. They had talked a great deal during the weeks they'd been at sea. Marianne thought he was an unusually fine man, discreet and loyal. She hadn't told Axel about her affair with Sam. Marianne and Axel were reconciled, and Sam didn't ask any questions.

Marianne and Axel were in love, and while the waves of the Aegean rocked them Axel Joachim was conceived.

Marianne had long dreamed of becoming pregnant. Her heart pounded with joy when she realized she was carrying a little life. Axel smiled when he received the news, lifted her up and set her down on the ground again. He was pleased, but pensive, and didn't say much.

Back on Hydra the days passed harmoniously. Marianne took care of house and home and felt the small kicks of new life in her womb. She took out her diary for the first time in half a year and began again to write down her thoughts and dreams.

3/7-59
Since last have there been loads of dreams, but since I didn't have you, little book, at hand I can't write them down now. We are going to have a child at last. And we are travelling to see John some time this month if all goes to plan. I can't get anything done these days when everything is so uncertain. But I'll take you along, little book.

Through long working sessions upstairs at his typewriter, Axel got a better handle on the novel, which now had the working title *Linedansen*.

Henrik Groth was Axel's permanent publisher and had also become a close acquaintance of Marianne. Axel and Groth had enjoyed very close contact during the work with *Ikaros*, and the two of them had corresponded by letter and telegram between Oslo and Hydra. Groth was now more sure than ever in the book. "The book is a stroke of genius and there hasn't been such a significant writer in Norway in a long time."[21] Groth felt that the title, *Linedansen* — *The Line Dance* — which punned on "Line," the name of the protagonist's love interest, was a distasteful play on words in such a weighty work as this. He said that Axel should call the book anything he liked except *Linedansen*. The publisher suggested *Line* — short and sweet — and that's what stuck.

In the fall of 1959 the book was printed and the launch approached. The Jensens headed north and moved into Cappelen's apartment on Majorstua Road. One evening, Axel, who was known for always making new acquaintances, invited a two-metre-tall man home for wine and talk. In the middle of the chat the guest rose and said, "I'm leaving." Before Marianne and Axel knew what was happening the man had walked right out the open window on the second floor. Axel leaped out of his chair and looked out the window but there was no one there. He ran out the door to try to find the man and see if he was injured, while Marianne went to bed.

A while later the doorbell rang. Marianne reckoned it was Axel, who had forgotten his keys, but outside stood the tall man. He wanted to let them know that he was fine. Glad to see that the man was alright, Marianne went back to bed while the guest sat waiting for Axel. From the bedroom she could hear the water running in the bathtub. When she awoke the next morning, the bath was full of water and wild roses. The stranger had vanished without a trace.

Marianne's father was very ill. She visited him every forenoon and the two of them took slow walks together through the beautiful grounds of Frogner Park. One was obviously pregnant and the other was short-winded and weak-lunged. Marianne experienced a tenderness toward her father that she hadn't felt before. He was going to be a grandfather and Marianne had, after all, not made such a bad job of her life — she was married and they made ends meet. Her mother was worn out by the demands of her job and caring for her sick husband. But, notwithstanding the scant leave-taking she'd granted Marianne when she went off to Greece, she was glad to be expecting her first grandchild.

During their stay in Oslo, Axel invited his mother down from Trondheim. He hadn't seen her since he'd been a little boy, and they'd had nothing to do with each other. When she came, he bought her a fur coat and rented a room for her at the posh Grand Hotel, down the street from the royal palace. Marianne was moved by his efforts. But the reunion ended with Axel being rebuked by his mother, leaving him wounded.

———

With the publication of *Line* Axel finally had money in his pockets so in October, when Marianne was six months along, they went to Stockholm together with Per and Else Berit to buy a car. Axel had lost his licence on account of driving drunk; the plan was for Marianne to drive their new car back to Oslo. Through friends they purchased a beige Karmann Ghia with light-brown leather upholstery — something altogether different than the blue Beetle that had taken them to Athens two years previously. All four of them stopped in at the home of Per's half-brother to spend the night there before driving the rest of the way to Oslo.

Marianne and Else Berit — both pregnant — shared a bed while the men sat up. Tired after a long day, Marianne pulled her brown velvet dress over her head, got under the comforter and fell right to sleep.

In the middle of the night Axel tumbled into the room, instructing Marianne to get dressed fast because they were driving home. He and their host had argued and Axel had been asked to take his wife and leave. Axel was furious and wanted to depart immediately. Marianne and Axel stood on the slate steps outside the house, arguing loudly. She held onto the iron railing and begged not to have to drive in the middle of the night, pleaded with him to calm down. Still enraged, Axel grudgingly agreed to postpone their departure until the next day.

Marianne felt powerless and unsafe when Axel lost his temper. Alcohol was nearly always a contributing factor when things spun out of control. He was easily offended and hard to handle when he had too much to drink. She breathed deeply until the tense situation exploded or fizzled out.

AXEL JOACHIM

As *Line* was about to be released, Marianne's father took a turn for the worse and was admitted to the National Hospital. His kidneys were failing after many years of coping with tuberculosis medications.

Marianne sat by his bed every day, with her round belly. The day her father told her to buy just one newspaper, rather than the three he regularly read, she understood that he didn't have long to live. He became weaker and weaker and at last lost his voice, squeezing Marianne's hand hard when he wanted to signal "yes" and more softly when he meant "no." Marianne's mother remained rigidly self-contained, her feelings tightly under wraps, but she bought a Valium for Marianne so she wouldn't weep.

One afternoon in November, Marianne's mother came out into the white hospital corridor and said that Father was dead. Marianne hugged her stomach and felt the little one turn and plant a tiny foot under one of her ribs.

While Marianne and Axel were in Oslo, Sam Barclay had been taking care of their house on Hydra. They needed new wind-tight windows now that the family was about to become larger. Mouldings were also missing along the ceilings and around the doors. Sam had engaged local workers and had promised that everything would be done by the time they came back with the baby.

With communication taking place by mail, it could take weeks before they heard from each another. Sam addressed his letters to Marianne; she was delighted every time she found an envelope with his writing in the postbox. She missed Hydra, feeling more at home there than in Oslo.

4.12.59
Hydra, Greece

Dear Marianne,

I am writing this from your little house on the hill. It is a lovely day, warm & sunny. It rained last night.

Fransisco has just been up to give an estimate for the work to be done . . .

I am sorry Oslo is so sad with cold and fog. Hydra has been lovely. I have not worn a jersey for some days now. . . . Anyway, I am glad you are in Oslo really because it will be better to have the baby there.

I am sorry about your father being back in hospital again. I hope so much that he will get better this time too.

George Johnstone is back in Hydra for a month over Christmas . . . He has just finished another book. Charmian's "Walk to Paradise Gardens" has been accepted in America and her "Peel Me a Lotus" (about Hydra) has just come out in England where it has had very good reviews. So they are fairly pleased with themselves . . .

What is Axel's new book that he has started? Is it Miracle Man or another one on the lines of the last one? . . .

I miss you both so much.

Love, Sam!

P.S. James is most excited about the sweater and so am I about mine![22]

The fall of 1959 was difficult. Marianne's father had died and now she saw Axel's head swelling with the success of *Line*. She stood by her husband's side when the book came out and made Axel famous. Young Jensen was the shooting star in the Norwegian literary firmament and everyone had an opinion about the new novel. The newspaper *Arbeiderbladet* wrote: "A profound, bleeding earnestness and an extravagant desperation and joie de vivre shines through Axel Jensen's great new novel." According to the reviewer, the talent Axel had shown in *Ikaros* was now in full bloom. The paper *Morgenbladet* opined, in contrast, that the book was banal, full of hectic swaggering and utterly devoid of even a glimmer of a mature thought or artistic value.

The book contained taboo words and descriptions of sexual intercourse and was judged immoral by a range of critics across the country. The large, influential newspaper *Aftenposten* refused to review the book because it was too racy, and the main public library in at least one county in Norway declined to add the book to its collection. Nonetheless, *Line* was one of the few Nordic novels to make the crossing to an English-speaking market, under the title *A Girl I Knew*.

While Marianne and Sam exchanged letters between Oslo and Greece, Axel and John corresponded frequently. John lived in El

Buen Retiro in Cuernavaca, Mexico, but it was just temporary: he didn't like the sound of the address.

> I've seen your idol Henry Miller several times of late. He is a much sweeter gent than one would guess from his stinking writing.
> I will be in Mexico for three months. After a brief period in Peru to unearth certain "things," I will try to stop in Norway en route to Egypt to see your magnificent child and beat the shit out of you. Your baby will undoubtedly be a genious. I will not beat him up. Nor Marianna. Only YOU.
> That I love you goes without saying.
> Marianna, too.
> Baby in woom, also.[23]

———

Axel Joachim was born on the 21st of January, 1960. Attending the birth, Axel senior saw his son enter the world. The baby boy had jaundice and looked like his father.

The next day Axel came to the maternity ward together with a close friend of Marianne. Marianne watched them, thinking that they were lovers. She didn't *know*, but she guessed that's what was going on. The visit made her so uneasy that she lost her milk and couldn't breastfeed the child, who was somewhat weak on account of his jaundice. The next day the midwife put a feeding tube down into the baby's stomach so he could be nourished. Five days later Marianne stood on the steps outside the clinic with the boy in her arms, waiting for her mother to fetch them. She couldn't help wondering about her and her child's future. Would they be alone in the world? Would Axel be there for them?

Marianne and the baby boy moved in temporarily with her mother, whose home provided a base for them while Marianne got back on her feet. Axel didn't stay in Oslo long. To avoid paying taxes to the Norwegian government he travelled back to Hydra a week after his son's birth. Marianne and Axel Joachim followed four months later.

———

When Axel collected them in Athens Marianne was unaware that he'd already found himself a new woman with whom he wanted to share his life. He had met Patricia Amlin, an American painter. Axel said nothing in Athens, but Marianne thought there was something peculiar about him — it was as if he'd become a stranger to her and the child. Marianne thought about how the overwhelming reception of *Line* had gone to his head and how she had seen little of him at the hospital. He hadn't been there for her and their baby, and now she had no idea what she was walking into.

Before taking the ferry to Hydra, they spent one night at a hotel and one night in a huge house along with some friends of Axel who were stationed at the American military base in Athens. Marianne was tired after the journey so Axel took care of Axel Joachim, carrying him in his arms and telling him how the stars were positioned in the sky the day he was born. He didn't prattle away in the high voice usually reserved for babies, but spoke seriously to his son as if he were a little professor. The child listened with big eyes and cried a bit. His father comforted him and carried him and talked until the little one fell asleep.

On their way through the port of Hydra the next day, laden with suitcases, diapers and baby, an old Greek woman they knew headed for them. She crossed herself, peeked into the baby carrier and dry-spat at Axel Joachim. Marianne's heart beat faster in her chest as she looked with astonishment at the hunchbacked woman. She didn't know that this symbolic gesture was the customary way of protecting a child from the evil eye.

At twenty-five years of age, Marianne came back to the little whitewashed house in Kala Pigadia with a baby in her arms. The house had neither electricity nor running water; it was a marked transition from Oslo. Marianne dragged the baby's carriage, an old one handed down to her by an American woman, between the house and the port. The Norwegian family attracted attention and the little blond Buddha was passed from lap to lap.

Axel said nothing about his new lover. Marianne didn't ask any questions. Foreseeing what was about to happen, she shut her eyes and hoped it would fade away, hoped that Axel would find contentment with her and their child. But the American painter with the long dark hair had rented a room on the island and spent more and more time with Axel. Marianne picked one of the yellow flowers on the un-cemented terrace and plucked off the petals one by one. In her mind she pictured the blue-painted wooden bench where they changed Axel Joachim's diapers, the white rooms, the books and typewriter. She was afraid of losing everything they had created together in this place. The fairy tale suddenly lay beyond her reach. It was as if there were a glass wall between her and everything else. In a dreamlike state, she saw herself climbing up on the wall around the house while she stared down the steep hillside, wanting out.

THE MAN IN THE SIXPENCE

One warm late morning in May, Marianne enlists a neighbour woman to watch Axel Joachim while she goes shopping. Bougainvillea vines are blossoming in pinks and reds; the whole of Hydra is about to burst into bloom. She descends the steep steps from the house and follows the old river course toward the harbour, greeting acquaintances along the way.

"*Yassou, pedi mou.*" Hello, my child.

"*Yassou.*"

Down at the port she goes into Katsikas' with her basket to buy bottled water and milk for the baby. She is wearing a pair of wooden-soled sandals and a home-sewn skirt with big pleats and colourful stripes against a pale blue background. A man she hasn't noticed before stands in the doorway, the sun behind him, in chinos and a shirt with rolled up sleeves. Tennis shoes and a sixpence cap. Marianne can't see his face, just his silhouette, and she hears him say, "Would you like to join us? We're sitting outside."

Marianne accepts demurely and finishes her shopping. She takes her basket and goes out and sits at his table, where three or four other foreigners are gathered. They sit on the small straight-backed chairs with woven seats. Some are drinking retsina. Marianne drinks juice, shying away from alcohol so early in the day. She is alert, aware that she must soon go home to relieve the babysitter. Bashful and not knowing quite what to say, she looks away. It's quiet and relaxed around the table. The man doesn't say anything remarkable, but he looks at Marianne. And when their eyes meet, her entire body trembles.

Marianne rises from the table and takes her leave. Walks with light steps up Kala Pigadia to the little house. The basket is heavy, but she is not aware of the weight. She feels almost tipsy when she comes home. She hustles the sitter out the door and puts on some music. Dances around the room, thinking that it's wonderful to be there together with Axel Joachim. Doesn't care that he doesn't want to go to sleep right away. Feeling light, easy.

Marianne rests during the afternoon with her child while the sun is at its highest. When she awakens she is full of anticipation. She wants to go down to the port again, where everyone she knows is gathered and where she may again encounter the Canadian whom she met earlier in the day. Leonard. The dark-haired poet with the sixpence and the intense gaze.

She pulls a sunhat on her baby boy's head and rolls the carriage down Kala Pigadia, Axel forgotten for a little while.

————

Leonard Cohen remembers that he'd seen Marianne many times together with Axel and the baby before she took any notice of him. He had watched them sailing down the port — blonde, beautiful and tanned — and he thought, *What a beautiful Holy Trinity they are.*[24]

It was more or less accidental that Leonard came to Hydra. He was staying in London to work on his first novel, but felt that it never stopped raining there. He was from Montreal, where it was snowy and cold, but people knew how to keep their houses warm. In London it seemed to rain ceaselessly and there was little warmth indoors. A hot water bottle took the chill out of the bed, but didn't banish the dampness that pervaded the sheets and his clothing.[25]

One day Leonard walked into the Bank of Greece, to cash a traveller's cheque or on some other errand. One of the tellers was a young, tanned man who was smiling. Leonard asked, "How did you get that expression? Everybody else is white and sad." The man answered that he'd just come back from Greece, where spring was in full swing. Leonard got on a plane to Athens the next day, the 13th of April, 1960. He visited the Acropolis, spent the night in Piraeus and took the boat to Hydra. He wrote his mother a postcard saying that he wasn't suffering from culture shock; on the contrary, he felt that Hydra was home.[26]

Leonard, whose mother was of Russian origin and whose father had been a military officer, had an old-fashioned background, like Marianne. They shared some of the same courtesies — values that belonged to an older era. Leonard's calling had been known to him from a young age. He knew that he wanted to be a writer, not for a popular audience, but for dead poets like William Butler Yeats. He wanted to be one of them. And if he could become a writer with that kind of integrity — if the the gift had been bestowed upon him — there would be money, and women. Not in great quantities, but enough. He would have a roof over his head and a beautiful view.[27]

The attractive and likeable Canadian was quickly included in the island's coterie of expatriates. He stayed with the Johnstons at first, until he found himself a small house that he rented for fourteen dollars a month. He lived on the stipend he had been awarded in Canada following the publication of his first book of poetry.

————

The island's foreigners often gathered at the port in the evening, the day's work behind them. One of these starry spring nights, the smell of flowers in the air, the usual gang is assembled at the back room of Katsikas'. Leonard Cohen is there. Marianne, Axel and his lover Patricia. In the light of oil lamps, they drink retsina from an oak cask. In the middle of the floor is an oval pan full of charcoal. Sophia hooks down a dried octopus from the ceiling and readies it for the hot grill. Marianne doesn't like to have Axel Joachim out with her in the evenings: the neighbour girl with the long dark braids is keeping an eye on the little boy, who is in his pyjamas, in bed.

Marianne is having trouble concentrating. Leonard, in his cap and tennis shoes, is sitting on one of the straight-backed chairs. At the same table, Axel and Patricia are drinking wine. The mood rises as long discussions unfold about art and life. Patricia is beautiful, as slight as a tiny bird. Marianne feels a stab in her chest but doesn't make a scene. She has almost become her own mother, who maintained that if a glass had to be smashed in anger, choose a mustard glass.

Axel becomes steadily drunker, and late at night the four of them go outside for some fresh air. Leonard, Marianne, Axel, Patricia. They lie down on the flat, smooth paving stones, resting their heads on a low curb. Look up at the starry sky. They are all in their mid-twenties. It's 1960, two and a half years since Marianne first came to Hydra. The harbour is quiet. There are no tourists, no restaurants blasting thumping music. Just them.

A little while later the group breaks up and they go their separate ways. Marianne and Axel start in on the ascent up to their house. There is tension between them, the run-up to a quarrel. Just before they reach home Marianne stops by a ledge and puts down her basket of food and milk. She asks Axel to leave, to take Patricia away from Hydra. "Go to her, go to Patricia, because that's where you'd rather be!" she says loudly and clearly, even though she doesn't really mean it. She has to get it out and can't remain passively quiet, ignoring the betrayal any more.

Axel is livid.

They argue loudly. There's some shoving and scuffling. Marianne tears herself loose and storms up the steps to the house. Axel rushes after her. Axel Joachim is alseep in a wooden cradle on the first floor; the babysitter hurries out when they come. Axel disappears into his workroom where his writing table is. Marianne listens as he discharges his fury. The chairs fly from wall to wall. He overturns everything he comes across, and begins to hurl things out of the window. Suitcases and clothes, hangers and books, hurtling out into the Greek night.

Marianne takes her child out of the cradle and positions herself behind the door in the hope that Axel will calm down. She is scared. When he doesn't show signs of settling down, she takes off, running as fast as her legs can carry her to the home of George and Charmian and bangs on the door, begging them to please help her. Marianne hands them the baby and asks if they will look after him while she hurries back home to check on Axel. She's afraid that he's going to do something. George and Charmian stop her and she lets herself be persuaded to stay with the baby, who is wide awake.

A short while later Axel comes running to the house, barefoot, in the ankle-length djellaba he wore in the Sahara. Standing there, sliced up and bloody from stepping on broken glass, he announces that he's there to fetch his wife and child. George calms Axel and leads him into his study. Charmian makes up a place for Marianne and the baby to sleep and bundles them to bed.

The next day it's blown over. Marianne and Axel bring the

window frames with broken glass to Francisco the carpenter to repair. The matter isn't spoken of again.

———

It hadn't been more than a few days after Marianne had met Leonard for the very first time when she realized that her relationship with Axel was disintegrating. She stopped pretending not to see Axel's lover. Axel had been with his little son for barely a week when he decided to take a trip to figure things out. He intended to discover whether he wanted to spend his life with Marianne or the other woman. He was leaving in his own sailboat, a BB11 that had been transported from Norway on a freighter and set on land in Piraeus.

It was a tearful parting. A group of friends gathered at the port to wave goodbye to Axel. Marianne had an urge to leap into the sea and swim after the boat — *despite everything there might be a wisp of hope*, she thought. Maybe he would find out that it was Marianne he still wanted. He had come back to her before, and they had, after all, exchanged vows of eternal fidelity when they married in Athens the year before.

Marianne recovering from
appendicitis in Lamia, standing beside
the car she and Axel drove to Athens.

Marianne and Axel's house in Kala Pigadia [TOP]. The Swedish writer Göran Tunström lived in the dark house to the left. Marianne would call to him from the terrace: "Time to eat!" The staircase in their house led up from the ground floor, where the kitchen and living room were [BOTTOM LEFT]. Axel's workroom on the second floor [BOTTOM RIGHT]. There was also a bedroom/living room on this floor.

Marianne and Axel pose
in their idyllic setting
for a Norwegian weekly
magazine [TOP].

Axel and dog on the
terrace of their house
[BOTTOM].

Marianne with newly dyed hair at the ancient theatre in Aydin, Turkey, during her travels with Sam Barclay [ABOVE]. Axel on Barclay's schooner, *Stormie Seas*, in the spring of 1959 [OPPOSITE]. Axel Joachim was conceived aboard the boat during this time.

Marianne at Katsikas', where she was filling her shopping basket the first time she spoke to Leonard [ABOVE].

The two oldest Hydriot women Marianne knew. The woman on the left offered infant Axel Joachim spiritual protection by ritually "spitting" on him upon his arrival to the island [LEFT].

Axel, Leonard, Marianne
and Axel Joachim in his carriage
at the back of Katsikas' shop, 1960.
[James Burke/Time & Life Pictures/Getty Images]

Lunch at the port shortly after Marianne and Leonard met. From the left: Marianne, Axel Joachim, Leonard, the Englishman David Goshen and the Australian writers George Johnston and Charmian Clift, 1960. [James Burke/Time & Life Pictures/Getty Images]

Marianne with American novelist Gordon Merrick (left) and Chuck Hulse (right) — or ChuckandGordon, as Axel Joachim called them. It was Merrick's birthday.

Bathing at Spilia, also known as swimming "on the rocks," 1960. Standing, from the left: Charmian Clift, George Johnston, Marianne and Leonard. Jason, the Johnstons' youngest son, was learning to swim.

Leonard plays his guitar at the taverna known as Douskos, 1960.
The circle of listeners includes Charmian Clift and George Johnston
(to Leonard's left), Axel (seated on the ground) and Marianne.
The little colony of artists and travellers often gathered there in the evenings.

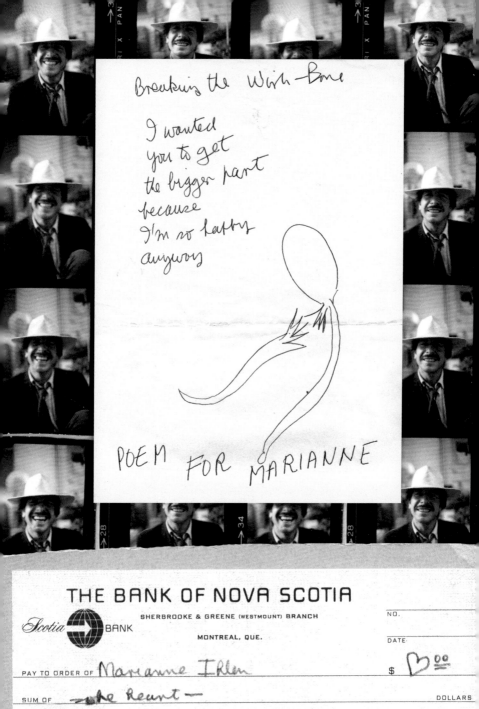

Breaking the Wish-Bone

I wanted
you to get
the bigger part
because
I'm so happy
anyway

POEM FOR MARIANNE

THE BANK OF NOVA SCOTIA

Scotia BANK

SHERBROOKE & GREENE (WESTMOUNT) BRANCH

MONTREAL, QUE.

NO.

DATE

PAY TO ORDER OF Marianne Ihlen

$ ♡ 00

SUM OF —the Heart—

DOLLARS

ACCT. NO. 4986

Leonard Cohen

SAVINGS DEPARTMENT

⑈00251⑈00 2⑈

Marianne at the
port of Hydra, 1962.

[OPPOSITE] Leonard mailed Marianne photo-booth strips
when they were apart. A poem from Leonard [TOP], and a heart,
transferred by cheque from Leonard to Marianne [BOTTOM].

Axel Joachim with a bundle of birds from a local hunter, spring 1962.

[OPPOSITE] Marianne and Axel Joachim loved to have their pictures taken in photo booths. Here are mother — with a fashionable bob — and son in Montreal [LEFT]. The photos at right show Leonard [TOP] and Marianne [BOTTOM] with Axel Joachim at Grafos' taverna, autumn 1962.

1962 AUTUMN

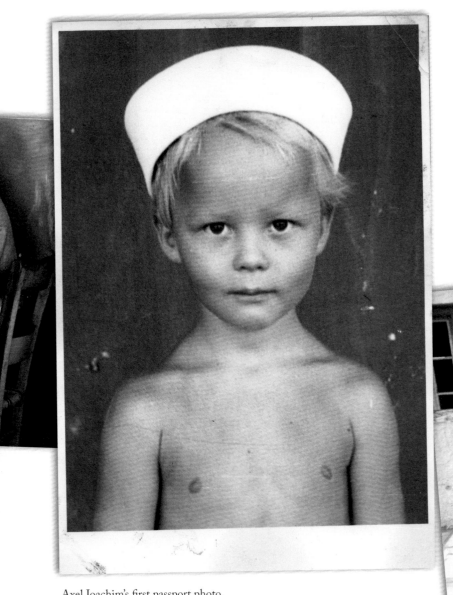

Axel Joachim's first passport photo.

Marianne and the mirror in which she and Leonard
contemplated themselves, wondering who they were; Marianne and
Leonard strolling at the port, 1963; Leonard sunning himself
on the terrace outside his study. [OPPOSITE, CLOCKWISE FROM TOP]

FEB · 63

HAPPY
MOTHER'S
DAY
FROM
AXEL
AND
LEONARD

Marianne and Leonard at home
on their terrace on Hydra [ABOVE].
[photo courtesy Aviva Layton]

Marianne and Leonard in Athens,
captured by a street photographer
in 1965 [RIGHT].

[OPPOSITE] Axel Joachim framed in a second-floor window of
Leonard's house [TOP LEFT] [photo courtesy Aviva Layton]; Leonard's close
friend and mentor the poet Irving Layton during a visit to Hydra
[TOP RIGHT] [photo courtesy Aviva Layton]. Greetings from Axel Joachim
and Leonard [BOTTOM].

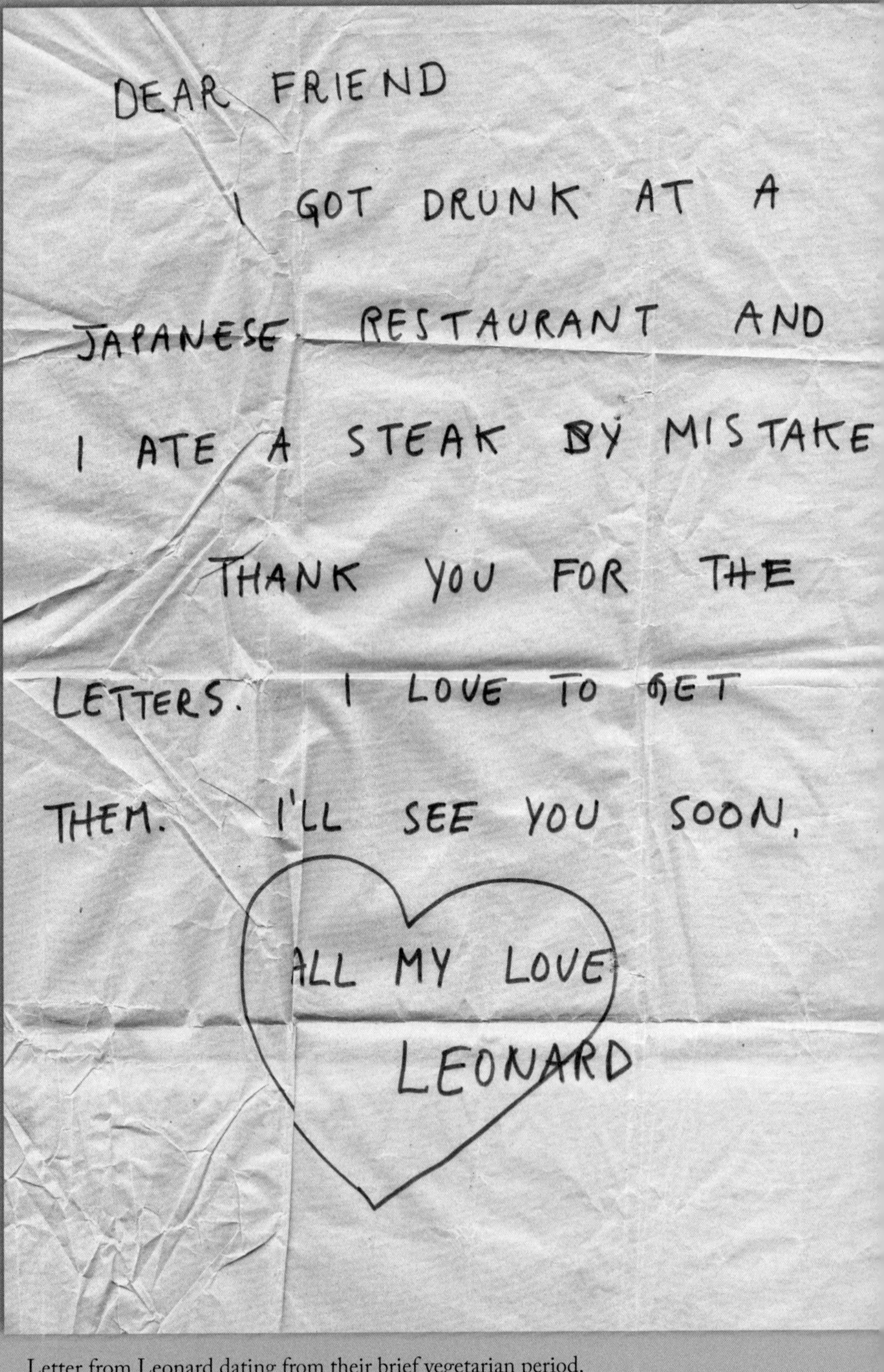

DEAR FRIEND

I GOT DRUNK AT A

JAPANESE RESTAURANT AND

I ATE A STEAK BY MISTAKE

THANK YOU FOR THE

LETTERS. I LOVE TO GET

THEM. I'LL SEE YOU SOON,

ALL MY LOVE

LEONARD

Letter from Leonard dating from their brief vegetarian period.

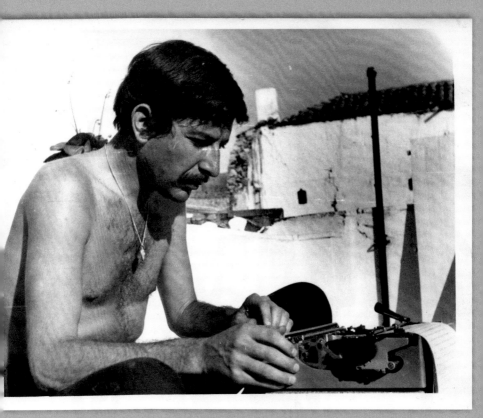

Leonard on his terrace, working at his green Olivetti.

Not having you is like feeling Spring begin over and over again

Marianne in the jacket Leonard had worn as a member of The Buckskin Boys. The band took its name from the jacket, which had been given to Leonard by his father [BOTTOM]. A note from Leonard [TOP].

Chapter 5

SLOW WALTZ

After Axel had gone, Marianne invited some friends back to the little house. They sat outside, drinking retsina and talking. She was in good spirits, choosing to believe that everything would turn out alright. It was the end of May and wildflowers were still in bloom. The earthen-floored terrace was blanketed with small yellow and white flowers. Observed by one of her guests — a young American whom she'd only just met — Marianne pinched off a handful of blossoms and placed them in an envelope. "I love you," she wrote on the note she slipped inside the envelope, which she addressed: *Axel Jensen, American Express, poste restante, Athens.* She knew he would have to stop in there.

She posted her love letter at the port the next morning. The young American happened to be travelling to Athens on the same boat as the letter.

A few days later the young man stood at the American Express office in Athens, waiting to collect his mail. In the neighbouring queue, a blond man accompanied by a beautiful woman opened the letter he'd received. Small flowers spilled out of the envelope. The American contemplated the stranger and the dried flowers that lay strewn on the floor and thought, *That must be the letter from Marianne, and this must be Axel.* He took the ferry back to Hydra, made his way to Marianne's house and said, "I just had to tell you, Marianne, that they are together." She realized then that it was all over.

Marianne felt utterly defeated. When she'd followed her heart to warmer climes, she hadn't envisaged for herself a life as a single mother in a foreign country, without income or a job to fall back on. Marianne had to make a decision about what she was going to do with her life. Not an artist, and lacking paid work of some other kind, Marianne's obvious course of action was to return to the north. Yet Hydra felt like home in many ways. There was the house, and she had good friends and neighbours who supported her.

And then there was Leonard.

The coming together of Marianne and Leonard was like a slow waltz. They began to meet during the day. He told her over and over that she was the most beautiful woman he'd ever seen. Marianne quivered, shaken by the patience and goodwill Leonard showed her and which she couldn't fully understand. She pushed away the pain Axel had inflicted on her and, for their child's sake, pulled herself together, just as her mother had taught her. Instead of cowering under the blankets, she danced the *danse macabre*, climbing ten metres up the cliff and diving between the rocks into the sea.

Leonard sat and watched her, took her in hand and led her home. Marianne wanted to block out all painful thoughts and lose herself in falling in love. When she joined in the Greek dancing and drank retsina, he waited patiently for her. She didn't want to stop dancing. She wanted to be beautiful and dangerous, to dance and dance until she escaped from herself. Leonard hardly touched alcohol himself, in contrast to many of the other party-loving residents of the island. Leonard looked on while Marianne danced. Waited. Afterward they went home together.

With Leonard, Marianne felt protected and cared for. He was Axel's opposite: whereas Axel had been erratic and explosive, Leonard was placid and unassuming. He was polite and somewhat old-fashioned, raised in a traditional Jewish family in Montreal. Marianne recognized in Leonard the manners that she'd learned at her grandmother's — the niceties that were rarely encountered among people of their generation. He was the kind of man who removed his hat when a woman entered the elevator.

Leonard stood by Marianne while Axel was off with Patricia. They went for walks along the island's coast. Protected by his white sunhat, Axel Joachim was pulled along in the funny old baby carriage over the stones to the little bay in Kamini, where the fishing boats lay close together and the beach pebbles were smooth and warm underfoot. They ate lunch at the ochre-yellow restaurant with red window frames. When the little boy took his afternoon nap, Leonard read her poems. He had published his collection of poetry — Let Us Compare Mythologies — four years earlier and had come to Hydra to work on his second book, which would be called The Spice-Box of Earth.

Marianne was house-bound in the evenings, when Axel Joachim had been put to bed. Leonard came to her. They sat on the terrace, taking in the view of the ocean. Leonard sang lullabies for the baby while Marianne sat in the rocking chair with a piece of rope tied to the cradle. After she rocked the little boy to sleep, the balance of the night belonged to her and Leonard.

———

Leonard: There wasn't a man who wasn't interested in Marianne, who wasn't interested in approaching that beauty and that generosity. She was a traditional Nordic beauty, but she was also very kind and very modest. One never got the sense that she played on her looks; it was as if she wasn't aware of how good she looked. The American painter that her husband had left with was also a very lovely woman. It was as if everyone was young and beautiful and full of talent — covered with a kind of gold dust. Everybody had special and unique qualities. This is, of course, the feeling of youth, but in this glorious setting of Hydra, all these qualities were magnified. They sparkled. To me everyone looked glorious. All our mistakes were important mistakes, all our betrayals were important betrayals, and everything we did was informed by this glittering significance. That's youth.[28]

———

On the 15th of May, 1960 Axel sat down at the typewriter in Tourkolimano, a neighbourhood of Piraeus known for its good yacht anchorage.

> I'm sitting here frying in my own fat and writing on your rival's typewriter. Everything I undertake (even with the most effective camouflage and emotional lubrication) will (in the eyes of the world, perhaps also in your eyes) have the unmistakable character of brutal insensitivity. And not only that. The unpleasant taste of overblown egotism. I am therefore not going to beg for forgiveness. Or even plead for understanding. What I have done, what I am doing, is as far beyond the common morality as is possible to be, but it is not without consequences. And not without desperation.
>
> . . . The worst thing about this rat-trap is that I'm inflicting suffering upon you. It is truly grievous if this is the result of the individualism that I believe in and live for, my conviction that one must hold one's head high in the world and not buckle under external pressure, not drown. The strange thing is that the more one removes oneself from the rules of the game and rediscovers one's inner morality, the greater the pressure becomes, the more intense the solitariness. Because your husband is not merely happily fleeing from responsibility; he is lonely — and he struggles. Or, better: the battle is within him.[29]

The day Axel sailed from Hydra — ostensibly to discover whom he wanted to spend his life with — he and Patricia had rendezvoused on the nearby island of Poros. It was all planned, explained Axel in his letter, to spare Marianne the humiliation she would have felt had Axel and Patricia openly left Hydra as a couple. Axel's intention had been to parcel out her suffering: little by little she would come to understand that he had chosen Patricia and that they intended to live together.

> My heart bleeds for you, to use one of those
> threadbare phrases that has lost its meaning through
> overuse, but believe me, my little wife, I feel for you
> and suffer with you — and there are a thousand voices
> in me that shout: get a grip on yourself, quit all this,
> go back home, hold her close to you and give her what
> she needs: you.
> Everything there (and Little Axel; naturally, he
> gnaws at me) oppresses me. But then there are other
> voices, other rooms. I wish so very much that you
> understood me, that you could feel a little for me in
> the way I feel for you, it would help me immeasurably,
> but I know that would be asking for the impossible.
> My conflict is so invisible, so egocentric — no, I must
> accept being alone with this.
> . . . Give my regards to no one. Think of me. I am
> (believe me!) so much more fond of you than ever
> before! And I admire you. And I *don't* say "love," out
> of fear of using a word whose breadth we don't truly
> comprehend.
> Live well, your own Axel[30]

Marianne had already gone through the shock of abandonment, tipped off by the young American who reported seeing Axel and Patricia together in Athens. The letter that now came from the typewriter of Axel's lover was just salt in her wounds. Any hope of getting Axel back had already died within her.

ACCIDENT IN ATHENS

While Marianne and Axel Joachim were on Hydra, Axel and Patricia spent a couple of weeks with an American friend stationed at the military base outside Athens. It was from this base that the Voice of America was broadcast, giving the foreigners on Hydra the latest music and big stories like the war in Vietnam and racial unrest in the U.S. George Lialios related the news from the Greek press and they all read the weekly *Athens News*, which reported international events. There were also new people steadily arriving to the island, bearing news and ideas. The small foreign colony on Hydra knew what was going on in the world before the news had reached Norway.

Marianne and the other expatriates on Hydra at the beginning of the 1960s lived far from the enormous upheavals that were taking place in the world, but they listened to the news and discussed the changes and rebelled in their own ways. In coming to Hydra, many were rejecting the values of their homelands. Some wanted to escape the pollution of the cities and let their children run free in the clean air. Others wanted to live out their sexual leanings without harassment. The first African-American Marianne met on Hydra was amazed at the lack of difficulty he encountered when looking for a place to rent there.

––––––

On the military base outside Athens there was often good company and drinking in the evenings, and after one of the many parties Patricia insisted on taking some of the guests home. The sun was rising as she drove back to the base through the farmland that surrounded the city. The Greek farmers had arisen at dawn and were about to begin their day's work when

Patricia came driving along in the Karmann Ghia.

Suddenly a farmer pops up in the road with his donkey and cart. Patricia avoids them but the car spins around in the middle of a bridge and crashes into the railing. She is flung out of the vehicle and lands in the dry riverbed, which is heaped with clumps of cement and junk from an automobile workshop. Slamming into this leaves scarcely a bone in her body unbroken. It takes ages before she is brought to the hospital.

The hospital in Athens is antiquated, even for 1960. The American painter lies bandaged from head to toe, but the nurses have failed to keep the bandages saturated with antiseptic: Patricia has developed gangrene and the doctors have amputated one of her thumbs. Axel sits by her bed for three days and nights and is falling apart. In desperation he sends a telegram to Hydra asking Marianne to come.

Marianne is at a loss, but Leonard says that he thinks she should go. He's been spending a lot of time together with her and Axel Joachim and is beginning to know them both well. Slowly, love has bloomed between them.

Never having changed a diaper in his entire life, Leonard promises to take care of the baby while she's away. Marianne feels like a child and an adult at the same time. She's yearned for someone to look after *her*; the thought of visiting the hospital to tend to her estranged husband and his lover is more than she believes she can cope with. But she does what she has been asked to do, as she has always done. Leonard moves in and is given a lightning course in the care and feeding of a baby. Marianne takes the next ferry to Athens.

Marianne doesn't recognize the tiny, thin body in the hospital bed. She is unable to feel sorry for the woman lying there, bandaged and unconscious. Marianne is most pained by Axel's condition: he looks like a living corpse. She stays for a couple of days, keeping vigil by Patricia so Axel can rest. She drips antiseptic on her rival's bandages, unsure if Patricia recognizes her the brief moments she surfaces. Axel is in despair, tormented by guilt and apparently in shock.

Meanwhile, on Hydra, Leonard cares for Axel Joachim the best he can. When he runs out of cloth diapers, he makes use of the linen napkins that Marianne's mother had sent as a wedding gift, along with the silverware and sauceboat.

Marianne was relieved to come home to Hydra, relieved and grateful that Leonard had been there for her. The sight of Patricia in her sickbed, and of Axel cracking, had been traumatic. She was racked by anger and hatred, despair and jealousy. But she was in love with Leonard. The basest and most uplifting feelings rioted within her, and she struggled to come to terms with them.

A new chapter in her life was about to begin.

———

In August 1960 Axel's publisher sent a worried letter to Marianne. It had been several months since he'd received a word from Axel and now he'd heard by chance that Axel was in Mexico. Uneasy for both Axel and Marianne, Groth asked if something had happened between them. He said that he hadn't felt particularly optimistic at the sight of Marianne and her little baby leaving to travel all the way across Europe to meet her "fire-spouting volcano who erupts unpredictably in all directions." Groth asked Marianne to write him a few lines to say how they were all faring.[31]

Groth's publishing house, Cappelen, helped Marianne through her economic straits when Axel left her and the baby. She received cheques worth about fifty or a hundred dollars that came with brief notes: "transmitting 250 kroner," "transmitting 500 kroner." Axel let Marianne and Axel Joachim keep the house in Kala Pigadia, and when they were later formally divorced he transferred ownership of it to her and their son.

Late in the summer of 1960 Axel returned to Hydra and rented a house where he could continue his writing. He had accompanied Patricia back to Chicago and then travelled around Mexico with

John Starr Cooke. He'd experimented with psychedelic drugs and contracted malaria. Back on Hydra, he wrote one of his rare letters to his father back in Norway.

> Hydra 1/Aug. — 1960
> It has been an extremely difficult period for Marianne, Axel Joachim and me. The rumours are already buzzing around at home, that's unavoidable, people have mouths to talk with so there will be a whirring of rumours and talking with mouths. And I have surely enough committed a series of necessary irresponsibilities, our marriage hangs by a thin thread, and time will tell whether or not the thread will snap. The whole thing is naturally my "fault," as usual, if we're going to use the word "fault" or blame, etc.
>   Marianne, who was slowly being initiated into this dangerous world beyond conventions, has grown into a complete little person. The process has been a little painful at times, but that's true for all of us. . . .[32]

Axel asked his father not to worry too much: they were young and their only way of gaining wisdom was to do foolish things. Patricia, who was being talked about as the serpent in Paradise, would be back from Chicago as soon as she could hobble along: then they'd see what rabbits fate would pull out of its top hat.

Shortly after Axel mailed this sign of life to his father, Marianne receives a letter from John in Mexico. He writes that he wishes Marianne were there with him, so they could discuss everything that's happened. John thanks her for the photograph of Axel Joachim and asks Marianne to send his date and time of birth, which Axel has neglected to give him. John wonders where "the wreck" Axel is now — he was in total chaos when he arrived in Mexico, but the bird had regained his wings by the time he departed.

It must be Godawful to be married to a man who
is a genious in unhooking other people's psychis —
Godawful and wonderful at the same time. I imagine
you've learned to be very calm and wise. ARE you? Or
are you putting on masks?
    If you are, let me give you some advice: no masks.
I should know. I donned hundreds of them and they
don't work.[33]

John is very happy to have received a poem Marianne had sent to
him: he'd had no idea that she was a poet, he writes. He hopes the
light of the Aegean Sea dwells in her, and that Axel has returned
to her.

———

The very last time Marianne saw Axel on Hydra was in 1962.
Marianne later learned that he'd been expelled from the island
because, in a drunken state, he'd pushed a policeman into the sea.
Axel later described this himself as a sad exit.
    It had been a long way to the bottom. Or, as Leonard Cohen
would later write: *Yes it's come to this, and wasn't it a long way
down.*[34]

Chapter 6

AUTUMN OF LOVE

When Marianne and Axel had boarded the train from Oslo that November night in 1957, they'd planned to spend a year in Greece. Two years had passed and much had changed. Axel and Marianne, now twenty-five years old, had parted ways. Even as her bond to Leonard grew stronger, she saw no other option than to return to Norway with her six-month-old child.

Miraculously, the Karmann Ghia, which had come close to ending Patricia's life, was virtually unscathed. The car had been registered in Sweden in Marianne's name the year before, and now she needed to get it back to Scandinavia to avoid having to pay import duties that she could scarcely afford. She didn't look forward to driving with Axel Joachim in the backseat for mile after mile all the way through Europe, and she wondered how she might send the boy to Norway ahead of her. Leonard was thinking of returning to Canada and he offered to make the long drive together with Marianne before flying home to Montreal from Oslo. The stipend he lived on was almost exhausted and he had to recross the Atlantic to earn money.

· When Leonard proposed accompanying Marianne all the way to Oslo it began to sink in for her that she meant something to him. They spent more and more time together, were friends and lovers, and the tension of the recent turbulent months seeped out of her body.

One morning when Marianne had been at the port with Axel Joachim they stopped in at Katsikas' shop on the way home, as usual. Nearby on the port, one of the brothers in the family that ran the business had started a taverna where he offered simple fare. As Marianne and the baby were passing the little restaurant, a cap on one of the tables caught her eye. It was emblazoned with the logo of the Scandinavian Airline System — SAS. Hearing the lively chatter, she went over and asked if they were from Norway. An entire airplane crew sat around the table. Marianne introduced herself and explained that she'd been living on Hydra for two years, but was soon returning north.

The SAS crew were friendly and seemed trustworthy. Marianne made a rapid judgement call: she set the six-month-old baby on the table and said, "This little boy is going home to his grandmother in Oslo, and he can't travel alone."

The crew were to fly back to Norway as passengers, and without hesitating they agreed to deliver the boy to Fornebu Airport in Oslo. For her little boy's sake, Marianne thought it was better for him to fly home to Norway than to sit in the backseat of the car as they drove all the way across Europe. She telegraphed home at once and asked if her mother would meet the child at the airport.

Mother stood at the ready to receive her grandchild and help her daughter the best she could. "If you need anything, you know where I am," she'd said to Marianne the evening she departed Norway with Axel. Marianne needed her now. Her mother quickly made the necessary preparations at home and dispatched a telegram back to Marianne saying that she could send "Micro" — the baby's Greek nickname — to Norway whenever she was ready. While Marianne's mother was at work, her cousin, who lived near the offices of the national broadcasting company, would look after him. The crib was ready, and all she needed to know was what kind of milk Axel Joachim took — the rest she knew.

Marianne's mother was glad that she wouldn't be making that long drive alone, and she assured her daughter that she could have her pick of well-paid office jobs when she came to Oslo.

A few days later, together with Leonard, Marianne went to the airport with her baby, clad in hand-me-downs from George and Charmian's children. Marianne was allowed to carry Axel Joachim all the way into the plane, where she turned him over to the purser and the stewardess she'd met at the taverna near Katsikas'. Marianne kissed her little boy goodbye and checked that his bottle, diapers and a change of clothing were all there. She felt that the baby had been in the centre of a maelstrom ever since he'd come into the world: what he needed was to settle into a stable situation.

When Marianne received the cable that let her know that the boy was safely in Oslo she could finally relax. For the first time in a long while she felt unencumbered and could think of herself. She broke down and let the tears flow. Having held herself together so long, she'd nearly forgotten what it was like to breathe freely. With the baby in the good hands of her mother in Oslo, Marianne and Leonard enjoyed a few weeks on their own.

Leonard rented a small house near the port and spent most of his time writing. He hammered away from early in the morning until late in the evening on the green typewriter he'd bought for forty pounds the day he'd arrived in England. Leonard had come to Hydra both to write and to study Greek culture and history. He was an avid student and took private lessons in Greek.

On the 27th of September, six days after his twenty-sixth birthday, Leonard bought himself a house on Hydra for one thousand five hundred dollars. He'd inherited a small sum and had enlisted the help of a friend — the Greek-American painter Demetri Gassoumis — to make the investment. Leonard hung his blue raincoat on a hook in the entry and placed his green typewriter in his workroom.[35]

Marianne divided her time between the eagle's nest in Kala Pigadia and Leonard's house. She felt secure and no longer held her breath as she had done with Axel. He had always demanded more of her than she could give, yet she had bound herself to him. Like an anxious animal, Marianne was ever on the alert for the next attack. She'd been walking on eggshells, but now she could feel the ground beneath her.

Their days together on Hydra were tranquil. Marianne was relieved that Axel Joachim was in her mother's safe hands and she wouldn't have to cart him across Europe. Whether she was going to return to Greece or what she would do with the little house in Kala Pigadia she didn't know. For many of the foreigners on Hydra, the barren island was just a stop on their journey. They migrated onward, always seeking new places in which to better realize themselves and their art.

Marianne and Leonard lived a simple, quiet, predictable life. A disciplined man, Leonard awoke with the dawn to work. In the middle of the day they shared lunch and a siesta, and on the warmest afternoons of that autumn they took their swimsuits to the little pebble beach in Kamini.

Daily life involved a lot of work. Just filling a pot with water demanded effort. They knew that every drop of water came from the rain. They brought it up from the cistern under the floor or bought water that was delivered on a donkey. It was a nourishing kind of toil that they enjoyed doing together.[36]

The days she arose early Marianne observed the Greek women, in full mid-calf skirts, on their way to the bakery to buy their daily loaves. In her way she was one of them, despite her Bohemian lifestyle — so remote from the traditional Greek Orthodox existence. She enjoyed making food, finding comfort in the day's routines and rituals and losing herself in the practicalities of maintaining a household.

As she had seen the Greek women do, Marianne prepared chicken by placing it in a round pan along with potatoes and vegetables. She carried the dish to the bakery, paid a few drachmas to have it put in the oven and fetched it a couple of hours later. Starting early in the morning, the baker fired the oven with bushes and twigs. Marianne inhaled the smell of juniper in the small room. Wielding his big wooden paddle with fluid movements, the baker filled the glowing oven with loaves of bread and dinner casseroles of various kinds, each with its slip of paper to ensure its return to its rightful owner.

Marianne learned how to keep food from spoiling in the heat. The butter was kept cool at the bottom of a brown glazed ceramic mug full of water. She made sure that Leonard had a fresh gardenia on his desk and the house had a woman's touch. She was housekeeper and muse. She knew what each moment required of her, like Momo, who had sung so enchantingly that her voice teacher proposed to her.

EPIDAVROS

Their common friend George Lialios was a fountainhead of good stories as well as being a living encyclopedia. Marianne experienced all of this in English and her competence in the language grew, but she remained shy in spite of this. She was a woman of few words, listening more than she spoke. Together the little band of friends read the ancient drama about Hecuba, the queen of Troy who had nineteen children. Marianne worked her way through the Greek tragedy, in which Hecuba avenges the murderer of her youngest son by stabbing out the eyes of the king of Thrace and killing his sons. The life and death drama struck Marianne to her core.

The friends decided to visit the amphitheatre at Epidavros to see the drama performed in Greek. Besides Marianne and Leonard, there were George and Charmian and their children, the American author Gordon Merrick and his partner Chuck Hulse, and the Swedish woman Lena Folke-Olsson, who would later have two children together with Axel Jensen. None of them had much money, but they scraped together enough to hire a traditional caïque to take them over to Napflio, in the northeast

Peloponnese. In Napflio they hailed a taxi and packed themselves into it for the thirty kilometre drive to the historic theatre.

Marianne had been at Delphi and had visited an old amphitheatre together with Sam during their sailing tour of the Turkish coast. Epidavros exceeded everything. The magnificent theatre dated from four hundred years before Christ, and could hold fifteen thousand spectators. The proscenium was lit by simple stagelights. In long white tunics, the chorus floated in from the wings as if their feet didn't touch the ground, while their voices carried out over the amphitheatre.

The night was velvety warm. Marianne sat close to Leonard. Enveloped by the dark she heard Hecuba whisper to her and the hovering white figures who sang directly to her heart. Marianne didn't feel the effects of sitting on cold stone until the performance was over several hours later. The little group tumbled out into the night with the rest of the audience, and rode in the taxi back to the blue and white caïque that awaited them in the harbour at Napflio. They unpacked food and wine from their woven baskets. Ate and drank under the stars while the night became morning and then sleep overtook them.

GOOD DAYS

One of the foreign couples that had settled on Hydra was Magda Tilche, who was Czech, and her Italian husband, who was nine years younger. Fleeing from Czechoslovakia, Magda had made her way to Paris with a French doctor. In Paris she opened a little club and met her Italian husband. Their son Alexander was a few years older than Axel Joachim. Magda was tall and gorgeous, with flaming red hair and colourful clothing. She wore exquisite stone jewellery around her neck and clinking silver bangles on her arms. The first time Marianne saw Magda she thought, *That's what I want to be.* The Czech woman became like an older sister to her.

Marianne and Leonard spent many mornings and evenings

sitting around the crooked tables at Katsikas' with Magda. Leonard sometimes played his guitar while he and Magda sang beautiful Russian–Jewish songs. Leonard had played guitar for as long as he could remember and had collected and studied folk music since he'd been a teenager. He'd learned to play the songs himself and loved them. In high school he and his friends formed a country and western band and music became the centre of his social life. They played in churches and schools, in bars and town squares.[37] On Hydra he played for Marianne and the little group of expatriates.

Their café table and its cloth were protected by a sheet of white paper. Leonard could spend nearly the whole night covering the paper with poems. One night Marianne took home one of the paper sheets. She read the line "Nancy wore green stockings" among the doodles and half-baked poems before she folded up the paper to the size of a napkin and tucked it away for safe-keeping among her diaries and other small valuables.

When Magda decided to turn one of the old boatbuilding workshops into a bar, everyone pitched in. They painted and sanded and sewed cushion covers, washed and polished and sang along as the radio blared and the workshop was transformed into the island's newest bar: Lagoudera. Two dinghies, left behind by the boatbuilders, were hoisted up to the rafters as a reminder of the building's former purpose. With Magda's savings used up, Lagoudera was at last opened to great fanfare. The nightclub became a regular gathering place for foreigners and Greeks.

When they wanted a break from little Hydra Marianne and Leonard took brief trips to Athens and the mainland. They drank coffee at Zonar's Café and at local dives, and let themselves be immortalized by the old photographer whose head disappeared under a black cloth as he snapped them with his big old-fashioned camera. Marianne and Leonard, smiling, arm in arm at Syntagma Square.

They collected their mail at the American Express office. Met Greek friends at a bar and stayed at their regular hotel, Niki 27, in Nikis Street, a simple and sparsely furnished hotel with two or three rooms on every floor. They picked up the key in the little brown reception area that reeked of sweat and rode the elevator up to their room, with its grey sheets that never saw the sun.

Usually they didn't make it further than Piraeus, where they strolled along the quay, looking at the boats and feeling the sun on their necks. Leonard in a white shirt and dark trousers, sometimes a dark vest. Marianne in a cotton skirt or dress, sunbleached strawlike hair falling to her shoulders. They shopped for food at the large open-air market, and found rare little treasures among the stalls of second-hand wares and antiques. Drank coffee at a Formica table at their regular restaurant, under flourescent tube lighting. Lodging at a dark hotel in a street behind the harbour, they could hear everything that went on in the neighbouring room through the thin walls. They slid under the sheet in the bare room and caught the boat back to Hydra the next morning at eight.

Both Marianne and Leonard felt the island was their home. Hydra was the first place where they'd spend any length of time after leaving their hometowns. Besides Larkollen, Hydra was the only place where Marianne had put down roots. Leonard had bought his first house here and he felt that he belonged in the philosophical climate by the Mediterranean Sea. It was as if the island had been waiting for them.

———

Leonard: I remember Marianne and I were in a hotel in Piraeus, some inexpensive hotel. We were both about twenty-five and we had to catch the boat back to Hydra. We got up and I guess we had a cup of coffee or something and got a taxi, and I've never forgotten this. Nothing happened, just sitting in the back of the taxi with Marianne, [lighting] a cigarette, a Greek cigarette that had that delicious deep flavour of a Greek cigarette that has a lot of Turkish tobacco in it, and thinking, *I have a life of my own, I'm an adult, I'm with this beautiful woman, we have a little money in our pocket, we're going back to Hydra, we're passing these painted walls.* That feeling I think I've tried to recreate hundreds of times unsuccessfully. Just that feeling of being grown up, with somebody beautiful that you're happy to be beside and all the world is in front of you. Your body is suntanned and you're going to get on a boat. That's a feeling I remember very, very accurately.[38]

———

Autumn was the most resplendent time of year on Hydra. The air was so clear that it seemed to Marianne, sitting by the sea and writing in her diary, that if she stretched out her hand she would touch the mainland across the water. Life was simple and was lived in the moment. Sex, love and the joy of being a human being sang within her as never before. She who had always felt so buttoned up was now untrammelled, walking freely. But it wasn't long before she was to return to Oslo and Leonard to Montreal.

Behind her closed eyelids an idyllic picture formed of all that was good in her life. The terrace carpeted with yellow flowers. The little wooden door that opened into the study. Axel Joachim sleeping, breathing evenly and packed snugly in a blanket in the rocking chair. The rope that led from the chair out onto the terrace, where she sat. Leonard reading a poem to her under the starry sky that wrapped around them. Layer upon layer of shimmering yellow stars. A donkey's bray slicing through the night. Remembering her grandmother explaining that she could make a silent wish on a falling star but she mustn't reveal it to anyone.

Leonard describes how he would sit on the steps, looking at Marianne while she slept with her golden hair spread upon the pillow: "I used to sit on the stairs while she slept, they were the most neutral part of the house, and they overlooked her sleeping. I watched her a year, by moonlight or kerosene . . . and nothing that I could not say or form, was lost. What I surrendered there the house has kept, because even torn wordless from me, my own first exclusive version of my destiny, like a minor poem, is too useless and pure to die."[39]

That was the autumn that Marianne and Leonard's spent on Hydra in 1960. She would always try to find again that autumn that sang so beautifully.

For M.

I stayed awake to see you sleep
Some faces die of sleep
Mouths go limp
Gone eyes leave a corpse behind
Maybe I could say goodbye
But you were perfect
You were whole
Your mouth was saying
I won't ever hurt you
Eyelids saying
Be alive be still
I got as far as the window
Something was wrong
The houses were too white
Cliffs too steep
What were the yards doing so clear
I wheeled around
I knew I had made a mistake
I tried to walk I ran
Everywhere I bumped my head
I was picking up prayerbooks
I kissed your sleep

1960
(Previously unpublished poem by Leonard Cohen)[40]

Chapter 7

BACK TO OSLO

It was November and Marianne was at last going to join Axel Joachim in Norway. She and Leonard enjoyed a good night's sleep at a nice hotel in Athens before setting out on the journey northward. More than three thousand kilometres lay ahead of them.

Before departing Greece, Marianne had the car checked to ensure it was in good order in spite of the hard knocks it had received. As soon as they put the car in gear and rolled out of the workshop, a fantastically tall Chinese man came running after the car, gesticulating with his arms.

"That's my car! That's my car!" he shouted.

"Ok, but it's mine now!" yelled Marianne back.

When the man didn't give up, Marianne and Leonard brought the car to a stop. Introducing himself as Mr. Tchang, the man hastened to the front of the beige car and opened the hood with a practised movement.

"Look at this! It's a Porsche motor!"

It turned out that Mr. Tchang was the son of an ambassador in Sweden and that he'd once been married to Marianne Bernadotte, who would later become the Countess of Wisborg. When the marriage dissolved, his ex-wife got the car, which she unloaded at a workshop in Stockholm. Marianne and Axel had had no idea that a Porsche engine lurked under the hood when they'd bought the car. With newfound horsepower, Marianne and Leonard zoomed off with a wave to Mr. Tchang, who was left dumbfounded by the brief reunion with his old car.

They drove through Yugoslavia, eschewing the major motorways in favour of the secondary roads that wound through poor farmland. They didn't hurry and slept at small inns along the way. Leonard remembers the drive as wonderful, though he also recalls minor quarrels. Marianne liked to drive fast; Leonard wanted to take it easy. Their disagreements evaporated when they stopped at little cafés and ate pasta or shared a hunk of bread and cheese or a bottle of wine.[41]

Marianne had longed for Axel Joachim after he'd gone ahead to Norway in August, but she'd also believed that it was safer for him to fly straight to his grandmother than to drive with her and Leonard through Europe. A light-grey baby carrier, full of things she was taking to Norway, lay on the backseat of the Karmann Ghia. Imagining that the carrier held an infant and that she could hear baby sounds coming from it, Marianne regretted her decision. She asked herself what kind of a mother she was to have sent her six-month-old baby away from her: he should have been here, with her.

A little apartment — borrowed from a French friend on Hydra — awaited them when they came to Paris. They decided to spend a few days in the city, to rest.

Some realities were inescable for Marianne. There were her feelings for Leonard, who was soon going back to Canada. She and Leonard hadn't discussed the future. Neither of them knew what was going to happen, only that they wanted to see each another again. There was a little child waiting for his mother, who had neither a job nor a husband to support them. When Axel left her, Marianne was scandalized at the prospect of a life without a father for her baby — it was almost unheard of, in her view. But she hadn't succeeded in putting that right.

Marianne climbed up into the windowsill in the white

bathroom. Huddled before the large window and its wrought iron bars, her body was racked with sobs as she thought how a jump would release her from all the pain. Leonard helped her down, holding her close until she'd cried herself out. Later she looked out over the roofs and church spires and contemplated her life, somewhere out there.

They strolled along the Seine in the evening light, pulling their jackets snugly around them against the cold wind from the river. Passed little stalls with wooden crates full of second-hand books and old comics. They visited the Louvre. Drank coffee in cafés and watched gentlemen in topcoats and ladies in trenchcoats and high heels. Felt the pulse of the city, a rhythm so different than Hydra's. Marianne closed her eyes and leaned her head against Leonard's shoulder, held his arm and let him lead her as if she were blind. She repeated the exercise several times, entrusting him to see for both of them while she slowly set one foot in front of the other, feeling that she had a firm footing before taking the next step. Finding her course and surrendering herself.

———

When they drove off the ferry from Kiel, they headed straight to Marianne's mother and Axel Joachim. Autumn had passed since Marianne had last seen him. She rang the doorbell and hurried up the steps with Leonard at her heels.

In a home-knitted jacket with mother-of-pearl buttons, knitted shorts with braces and laced leather boots, a shy tot stood in the entrée, waiting for his mama. When Marianne and Leonard came in the door Axel Joachim ran to his grandmother — whom he called Meme — and grabbed her leg while he stared wide-eyed at Marianne. His grandmother went over to the small piano in the living room and picked up the framed photograph of Marianne that she showed him whenever they talked about his mama.

"See, Little Axel — Mama."

Nonplussed at the presence of both Meme and Mama, Axel

Joachim screwed up his courage and slowly approached Marianne.

Leonard asked if they could light a fire. The red brick fireplace was almost never used, but Marianne's mother got moving and built a fire for the polite young Canadian who had escorted Marianne all the way from Athens to Oslo. Marianne's mother didn't speak English, but as a young lady she'd gone to private school in Paris. Leonard had grown up in Montreal. They mustered their French and conversed with one another.

Later that evening Leonard took his leave like a well-bred man. He checked into the Viking Hotel near the Central Station and settled into a little room facing the back garden for the few nights he would spend in the city.

Axel Joachim slept in Meme's room. Instead of moving the baby over to Marianne's girlhood room, Marianne slept in her father's old bed, her mother on the other side of the room in her bed; in the middle was the child's bed. The change was too great for the little boy and in the end Marianne went to sleep in her own room while Axel Joachim stayed with his grandmother.

Both Marianne and Leonard had houses on Hydra, but neither of them knew when or under what circumstances they would return to the island. Leonard had to go to Canada to make money. He couldn't live on writing poetry and he had several projects he wanted to try to make a go of when he got there. When Marianne and Leonard kissed each other goodbye outside her mother's house neither of them knew when or how they would meet again.

———

Shortly after Leonard left, an airmail letter from Axel arrived out of the blue:

Hydra, November 1960

Dear Marianne and Little Axel,
    It's night and I'm sitting behind my writing

appliance, pecking my way through existence, pecking myself into the strange world that the new book is miraculously turning into. The great art of letter-writing is not mine for the time being. Thank you for your letter. It is night on this island of ours and two lamps are burning, it smells of them, and my head is tired and I'm thinking of Little Axel and you, and it brings light and movement in this tired brain. When I come to Oslo in February he'll be walking, won't he? And he'll have a head of hair? God, I'm sitting here and it's night and the lamps are smelling and I'm a pretend family man and have left so much to you. But what else could I do than to write this book? Everything else is just a waste of time. Comical and posturing. So I'm writing a book.

Nothing has changed between Patricia and me. She's on the road to recovery, but is constantly having plastic surgery. We hope to meet again in February. Take care of the boy-child, who has his father's eyes. I shall be a peculiar father for him and a strange kind of husband to you — remote and scented with bitterness, but in any case unconventional. And that's something.

Until the next letter . . .

Axel[42]

Marianne was as tired of Axel's whinging as he was of hers. So much had gone wrong for them. Everything they touched became a shambles.

LONELY IN OSLO

Mother wanted Marianne to wear her coat of black Persian lamb and to get a permanent in her hair so she would look more ladylike. Marianne's return to Oslo and the winter she spent there were difficult. The town felt unfamiliar, and her old friends had scattered. She had the feeling that her mother had taken over her life and that she couldn't get a grip on things and establish an independent existence for herself and her little boy. She longed for the freedom of Hydra — faded batique and going barefoot — and wrote desperate letters to Axel, who sat in their house in Kala Pigadia, working on his book while he waited for Patricia to come from Chicago after her operation.

Axel was the only permanent link Marianne had to Hydra. Through six years they'd weathered many storms together, and he was the father of her child. The fighting and his abandonment of her had faded in her memory. She thought that in spite of everything it would be better if they lived as a family on Hydra than if she stayed in Oslo with a child that her mother had more or less taken over. Her heart belonged to Leonard but it had been several weeks and she had yet to hear from him. Feeling alone, she wrote to Axel and told him what she was going through. She raised the question of whether they should try to live together again, for Axel Joachim's sake. She put pictures of their eleven-month-old son into the envelope, along with cigars — a Christmas present.

On one of the days between Christmas and New Year's Eve, a reply arrived in the mailbox, postmarked on Hydra three days before Christmas:

> In all haste . . . I implore you in God's name not to
> send any more floods of tears in my direction because
> I'm the last person in the world who can comfort you.
> Try to understand and accept once and for all that
> there can never be an absolute relationship between
> us — and it is an absolute relationship I want to have,
> or no relationship at all. I know how much pain you're
> in, and it's tearing at me because I could assuage that
> pain of yours — for a little while. And then it would
> be more of the same. So stop. Stop! Stop!

Soon I won't have any other recourse to lessen
your pain than to give you a hard slap.

I think of Little Axel, and in general I think a lot,
but who am I to air all these feelings? Take my silence
for what it is. I'm sitting here on an island, and I feel
helplessly alone, and everything that means anything
to me is spread to the four winds. The book is
worthless in its current form. I've put it aside and am
reading night and day. Haven't heard anything from
Groth, but it's not his responsibility to write the book.
I'm very low, not a good state in which to write letters.
I'm writing this because you should know that I'm still
alive and that I'm marking Christmas in my own way.
I can't write more, for whatever I say or write will be
hurtful, or if it isn't hurtful would be just a temporary
anaesthetic, and I refuse to look upon you as a patient.
Liberate yourself from all this, Marianne. Live from
your own centre and find yourself a man who does the
same. We'll talk when I come to Norway. If this letter
seems harsh you know why. I'm sitting in a rat trap
and can't do more than snarl.[43]

On Christmas Eve, three days after Axel had composed his
letter to Marianne, Leonard sat before his green typewriter in
Montreal and did the same. The tone was completely different:

December 24, 1960

Montreal, Canada
. . . Tonight Montreal is very still under the snow.
The trees outside my window are black. The wind has
blown the snow from their limbs. Down the street,
in a basement of one of the great Victorian houses, I
think Jesus is about to be born. No one will ever know

except a few gentle animals, a couple of donkeys
and a cow, which are wandering towards us on the
Laurentian highway.

. . . I think we will see each other soon. I don't like
an ocean between us. . . .

There are a lot of possibilities. I have applied
to the government for another grant. There is a
good chance that I'll get it. Also, and this is more
important, Irving Layton and I are working very hard
on a series of television scripts. We're both overjoyed
with the progress we're making. He comes down here
every day and we write like mad.

Our collaboration is perfect. We want to turn the
medium into a real art form. If we begin selling them,
and I think we will, there will be a lot of money. And
once we make our contacts we can write the plays
anywhere. We'll all go to Spain or Greece and set up a
little writing factory. We both have excellent reasons
for making the venture a success. He lost his teaching
job because of his revolutionary ideas and I need
money to cross the ocean.

. . . When my poems come out in March I will
probably go on a reading tour across the country.
Maybe you could come with me. Television plays may
be the solution. Irving and I think that with three
months of intense work we can make enough to last
us at least a year. That gives us nine months for pure
poetry. It sounds like a good life.

. . . Mahalia Jackson is on the record player. I'm
right there with her, flying with you in that glory,
pulling away the shrouds from the sun, making music
out of everything. Send me pictures of you and Barnet
[the child]. Say hello to your family. Tell me what you
are feeling.

I give you all my love.

Leonard[44]

A few days later another letter came from Axel, begging Marianne to forgive the heartlessness of his previous letter. He doubted the worth of his manuscript, raged against it and left off work on it. He hadn't heard a word from Groth and assumed that his publisher didn't like what he'd seen of the book so far. Axel hoped sincerely that Marianne would rise out of her depression, for the sake of both of them. He concluded the letter by saying that she must stop measuring things by his yardstick and learn to use her own instead.

———

In the new year — 1961 — Axel's book *Line* was made into a film. Movie-goers flocked to see Margarete Robsahm topless as Line and Toralv Maurstad in the role of Jacob. Many had thought that Marianne should have played Line, but Axel hadn't been pleased with the suggestion.

The film concerns Jacob, a young seaman plagued by bad nerves. Under the advice of a doctor, he's travelled back to Norway to clear things up with his father, whose tyranny is at the root of Jacob's mental state as well as his mother's psychiatric condition. Back home, Jacob runs into Line, with whom he had fallen deeply in love before going to sea. They embark upon a love affair, which is impeded by parents and previous lovers. The film raised questions about the degrees to which environment and heredity determine choices made in adulthood. Marianne recognized herself and Axel in the dramatization of *Line*, which evoked memories and made her feel near to Axel again. She'd witnessed the entire writing process on Hydra, had read the manuscript and marked her red dots in the margins, had carried the sheaf of papers under her arm up as she walked up the narrow steps to the second floor, where Axel hammered out new pages on the typewriter.

The film received mixed reviews but was chosen to compete for the prestigious Palme d'Or at the Cannes Film Festival.

————

It was January 1961 and Marianne was still without work. She hadn't heard from Leonard since the letter she'd received after Christmas. Axel hadn't seen his son in half a year; all told, he hadn't spent more than a couple of weeks in the company of his child. As the little boy's first birthday approached, another letter from Hydra landed in the mailbox. Marianne had hoped that Axel would come home for the christening on the 19th of February, but when she read the letter she realized this wasn't going to happen: Axel said he wasn't coming to Oslo after all. Patricia was expected on Hydra at the end of February, if her lungs didn't collapse after the last operation. He'd finished writing the first part of the new book, which he was calling *Joacim*. But his chief reason for writing was to congratulate their son on his birthday. Axel suggested to Marianne that they should give the boy a new name before the baptism. He was afraid that bearing the name Axel would harm the child, that he would always live in the shadow of his name. He proposed Anders. In another letter soon after, Axel wrote:

> . . . And Leonard writes for Canadian TV? And you're
> still going around sniffing at each other, trying to
> make up your minds. Yes, yes.
> Can you send me his address? I want to write to
> him to chew him out for not sending me a sign of
> life.[45]

They were each waiting to be reunited: Axel on Hydra with Patricia in Chicago; Marianne in Oslo with Leonard in Montreal. None of them had a clue about the direction their lives would take.

Chapter 8

UNEXPECTED VISIT

Sam Barclay hasn't forgotten Marianne after those idyllic weeks in 1958, when they were together aboard his sailboat. He sends a letter to Oslo proposing that she return to Greece and work on the boat the coming summer: she's looking for work and he needs someone to cook and serve his guests. Marianne sees this as a chance to get away from Oslo, but she recognizes that it would be virtually impossible to take Axel Joachim with her and she doesn't want to leave him with her mother again.

Leonard was keen for her to come to Montreal, but this depended on his job situation, which was uncertain. He let Marianne know that he didn't intend to stand in the way if she and Axel tried to repair their marriage. Perhaps there was no place for him, or for Patricia, in this predicament — he didn't know. All Leonard knew for sure was that Marianne was important to him and that the autumn they'd spent together on Hydra had given him courage and strength.[46]

Sam had spent Christmas in England and decided to visit Oslo before returning to Athens. Blond, tall and sinewy, he stood on the steps and waited while Marianne ran down to open the gate. He arrived in the undyed wool sweater that Marianne's mother had knitted and which Marianne had sent him the year before. It was strange to see Sam here in her own city, far from the sunshine and the tang of the sea that had permeated their coexistence on the

Stormie Seas. From his duffel bag he dug out an old captain's watch that he wanted Marianne to have. He fastened the handsome pocketwatch and its silver chain to her blouse.

Sam was there for several days. He slept in the guest room and played with Axel Joachim. At the harbour he took a look at Axel's sailboat, which had been transported back to Norway. And he attended to Marianne's mother — who had now met her daughter's second admirer from Hydra in less than two months.

One day as Sam sat on the green sofa, he looked at Marianne and asked, "Will you marry me, Marianne?"

He was in love with her. Now that she was single he nurtured the hope that he could persuade her to come back with him to Greece. He matter of factly made his case that marrying would be a good solution to their solitude. He promised to be there for her, always. They could sail in the summers and live on the mainland during wintertime.

Marianne felt she couldn't risk marrying the wrong man again and she declined. She was in love with Leonard, not Sam, and this time she wasn't going to be steered by practical considerations. Agreeing to become Mrs. Jensen hadn't been wise — she'd known that intuitively, but she'd believed that marriage would solidify her relationship with Axel. She couldn't have been more wrong. If she were to marry again it would be for love and not because she needed to be taken care of.

Sam and Marianne parted as good friends. Marianne entrusted him with letters and pictures, dried herring and sardines to deliver to Axel, and waved him off as he left for Fornebu Airport with his duffel bag slung over his shoulder. She sat at her writing desk — still plastered with old photographs — and composed a letter to the suitor who'd just flown off to Greece. She wrote that everything was different after Hydra, that something had changed inside her. It was Leonard she loved, and she couldn't keep the captain's watch, which bound her invisibly to Sam.

Not long afterward came a letter.

Yacht "Stormie Seas"
Spetsai, Greece
Sunday. 11th

. . . Oh, Marianne! What a silly sort of letter to write.
You write as though it were the last you were ever
going to write. And you talk of giving the watch to
James?

I gave that watch to you, Marianne, because I
loved you and I wanted you to have it, not because I
wanted to bind you in any way. I will never have, and
never want to have, a hold on you in any kind of way.

Keep the watch. And weather you like it or not
you are always going to have me too because I am your
friend. Just your friend. And you may break the watch
into a million pieces or give it to who you please. It
will make no difference.

. . . I am glad that you have decided to stick to
Leonard. I knew you would even though I tried hard
to sweep you off with me. You would not have been
worth much if you had come, you know?

I wish you luck with Leonard. He sounds nice. I
wish I knew him better. Go right ahead with him,
Marianne. Maybe he will make you happy. But you are
wise now and what can I say?

I am so glad you are coming out of your cocoon. It
was not the deep freeze, for you have been growing
inside all the time. I am sorry Axel never had the
chance to see and know you as you are now too.
But Axel experiences people like an adventure or a
journey, and passes on. . . .

The sheep have just gone by along the edge of the
harbour, their bells jingling. A donkey is braying. I
suppose he is in love but he doesn't sound very joyful.

Stormie Seas is lying deserted, very calm outside the
window. The sun has gone down. It will be a new day
tomorrow.
I'll write to you again tomorrow, Marianne.
God bless you,
Sam
There is so much I have not said.[47]

Sam wrote letters in the form of a journal to Marianne, often
over the course of several days, before posting them to Oslo. He
wrote about life in Greece, common friends, wind and weather,
a little flower he'd found while out for a stroll. He wrote about
his feelings for Marianne. Their close friendship deepened. She
wanted him to be Axel Joachim's godfather, a duty Sam accepted
with pride.

Both Sam and Axel ask after the boy in their letters to
Marianne. A dejected Axel writes that Patricia isn't coming in
February as planned. He claims to have lost the ability to be
impatient and is astonished at his own fortitude. All suffering is a
kind of sentimentality, which he abjures. Pleasure is worthier than
suffering, he's decided — it's just a matter of living accordingly. In
closing, he writes:

AND THIS IS IMPORTANT. CAN YOU
INVESTIGATE IMMEDIATELY HOW WE CAN
GET A DIVORCE AS QUICKLY AS POSSIBLE?
PATRICIA AND I WANT TO MARRY AS
QUICKLY AS POSSIBLE.
You may think this sounds strange but I would
like to give her the sense of security to which every
woman is entitled when she gives herself to a man. A
sense of security that I have so deplorably failed to
provide you.[48]

Glad that her daughter was going to divorce Axel, Marianne's mother became more involved in the proceedings than Marianne herself. She made sure that Marianne would receive the economic support for her son to which she had a right. Living under her mother's roof and financially dependent on her, Marianne let her take over all the practicalities. For a speedy divorce one of them had to sue the other in court. It was decided that instead they would let the legal separation period run its course.

Marianne wrote to Axel on the 18th of Febrary, informing him that the separation papers had been signed but that the divorce would not be finalized for another year. She missed Hyda, she told him briefly, and it had been an eternity since she'd last heard from Leonard.

A fortnight later, Ess-Film hired Marianne as production assistant and substitute script girl for the film *Tonny*. It was based on Jens Bjørneboe's novel of the previous year — *Den Onde Hyrde* — in which he attacked the Norwegian prison system. Marianne had never read anything by Bjørneboe but she was happy about her new job, delighted that someone had use for her. Axel Joachim was in daycare at his grandmother's workplace while Marianne was at her job, and the two women shared childcare responsibilities between them.

———

Letters arrived from Leonard. They wrote to each other about meeting in Europe or Marianne moving to Montreal when she got on her feet. Axel informed Marianne that he'd sent Groth a draft of his manuscript to his fourth novel, *Joacim*. He was still waiting for Patricia. He thought that Leonard was a fool for not giving himself to his woman: he who doesn't give himself becomes stingy, Axel observed.[49] Marianne replied that she was a coward to have taken off so quickly, but the fear of being alone had conquered her. Now she yearned to be free of her mother's interference.

Thinking constantly of the autumn they shared on Hydra, Marianne longs for Leonard. It would be meaningless to go back to Greece, to an island full of memories, without him. Leonard is trying to save enough money to return to Europe, but poetry is no goldmine.

Two years after the publication of *Line*, Axel is in the house in Kala Pigadia, close to wrapping up *Joacim*. Marianne is curious about the book — created under their roof on Hydra — and contacts Groth so she can read it. Axel has again written about a young man searching for meaning and substance in his life. The protagonist Joacim is an advertising executive and a family man, married to Cecilie. At the start of the novel Joacim breaks with his job and his family and travels to Greece to realize himself as an artist. There Joacim meets a Danish student with whom he starts a relationship. Axel had written his protagonist into a dilemma, caught between social obligations and the desire for self-realization — a theme not unfamiliar to him or Marianne. There were other recognizable elements, prompting Marianne to wonder if she had been the model for Cecilie and if it was their life on Hydra that Axel had written about.

Hydra 13/6/1961

What's the new book "Joacim" about, well it's not about "what we have together." Cecilie resembles you as little as Line did, even less. Believe me or not, but if I were to make a portrait of you I'd do a better job than this.

That one part of it takes place in Oslo and the next three parts take place in Greece is true. But these are the settings I know; I can't write about other settings. What you have to understand is that this isn't an attempt at autobiography or self-revelation. I've just written a novel in the first person again, doing it as well as I could.

To be honest: I find it a bit difficult to write to you. I fumble for words, want to say something about Little Axel but feel that I lack the words. The whole thing is painful and sad and I bear most of the blame myself. The way things are now, I'm trying to stake out a new life for Patricia and me, and I hope to God that you find a man who deserves you.[50]

Like *Line*, *Joacim* aroused strong reactions. Several reviewers objected to the book, and Axel was criticized for maintaining too little distance from his characters — a charge he denied. Others contended that the book lacked perspective and depth and that the influence of Knut Hamsun was embarrassingly strong. The assumption later became widespread that Axel had based the figure of Lorenzo on Leonard Cohen, but the author himself countered that Lorenzo was modelled on Göran Tunström.

Contracted to the film production company until October, Marianne was involved in the pre-production, shooting and post-production work on *Tonny*. At the end, the director Sverre Gran wrote a testimonial for Marianne, affirming that her interests in art and literature were comprehensive and that she possessed a sound appreciation for artistic quality, as well as valuable language and writing skills.[51]

Marianne thought about Leonard every day. Around her neck hung a small Star of David that he had given her. Inside an oval locket decorated with small flowers against a white background she placed a little lock of hair and a photo of Leonard in one side and one of Axel Joachim in the other side. She often looked at pictures from Greece. She and Leonard smiled at the camera on strips from passport photo booths. Laughing. Serious. Marianne reread his poems to gain a deeper understanding of the man and his heart. She sustained long conversations with Leonard in her head, lost herself in daydreams and wrote English letters in her diary:

Darling,

I am so tired and work so hard all day. All alone
tonight looking at the moon and the sea. Will I ever
see you again?

ps. Driving home this evening I saw a falling star
landing. I said your name.

In the autumn of 1961 a telegram came from Montreal: "Have
house. All I need is my woman and her son. Love Leonard."[52]
Marianne was more than ready to pack her suitcase and leave
Norway.

Chapter 9

MONTREAL

Marianne's bags were practically already packed when Leonard cabled to ask if she and Axel Joachim would come to him. She'd been waiting for this. Brimming with anticipation, she settled herself and her eighteen-month-old son, who'd just said goodbye to his grandmother, into their seats on the plane. Marianne and Leonard hadn't seen one another in several months when she and Axel Joachim landed in Montreal. Leonard remembers seeing them through the glass, Marianne in her fur coat and a heavy valise in each hand. He waved. Marianne's hands were full so she waved back with her foot.[53] In love, her heart thumping, she led Axel Joachim through to the public arrivals hall.

Leonard had found lodgings for them in a grand old house in downtown Montreal. The façade of the townhouse was interrupted by a carriage gate that led from the street to the courtyard and the old stables, now converted to apartments. It was in one of these that Leonard had rented the third floor through his friend Robert Hershorn, who was one of Montreal's richest young men and who lived in the main house.

Marianne and her child first, Leonard following with a bag in each hand, they went up the stairs along the outside of the building and walked into the open, sunny living room with a view over the city and the Saint Lawrence River. As the sunlight warmed her skin, Marianne reflected on the turn her life had taken.

Leonard came from a conservative Jewish family, but Marianne and Axel Joachim were nonetheless soon introduced to his mother, Masha. His father had died when Leonard was just nine years old. Eccentric and handsome, Masha now lived alone in a great house in the wealthy residential area of Westmount. Marianne felt that her new "mother-in-law" took her in like a daughter.

During their first visit to Leonard's mother in Westmount, he took Marianne up to his old room on the second floor. He opened up one of the desk drawers and lifted out a box, which he placed on the palm of one hand while he took off the top. In the box lay two pendants: a miniature gold ballerina in a tutu and a little gold key. Leonard had been given the key as a high school graduation present. He bought a gold chain for Marianne and fastened it, along with the two charms, around her neck. Marianne later learned that it was customary to bestow a golden key charm on one's first love.

Marianne felt at home in Montreal at once. She could speak English, and even though Montreal bustled with millions of inhabitants and a multitude of cultures, the city wasn't so very different than Oslo. Still, settling into a big city with a toddler, without daycare or work, was a significant transition for Marianne. It was a far cry from Hydra, where she had friends and children ran freely in the streets and from house to house. Her world in Montreal comprised Leonard, the child and herself.

In the middle of the living room of their apartment was a big bed heaped with cushions. When Marianne came down with influenza she moved there to avoid infecting the others. Sensing that she needed a change from lying there and staring into empty space, Leonard bought her a yellow writing pad with light green lines. Marianne began to write. She wrote and wrote — about her grandmother and life in the large house by the shore at Larkollen.

Reverting to her childhood, she wrote like a seven-year-old, with capital letters. On the cover of the yellow notebook she penned "My Grandmother's House." After reading it, Leonard took the notebook with him when he went to New York to meet his publisher. The publisher contacted Marianne and asked if she was interested in trying her hand at a book: if so, he encouranged her to set to work at a typewriter. When Marianne tried to follow through, the flow of words dried up. The ideas filled her head but they refused to be turned into words on typewriter paper. The manuscript lay there and came to nothing.

Marianne fantasized about studying art and literature at McGill University, Leonard's alma mater, had she lacked the necessary qualifications from Norway. Leonard worked on his projects with his usual intensity. His second book, *The Spice-Box of Earth*, had just come out, making him known in Montreal's literary circles. He concentrated on a new manuscript that he was writing for Canadian television, and collaborated on a documentary film with artistic friends.

The little family was often in the company of Leonard's friends Irving Layton and Morton Rosengarten. Irving, a revolutionary poet and philosopher, had taught Leonard at McGill and had visited Hydra. He was a mentor for Leonard, who was his junior by twenty years. Morton was a sculptor and an old schoolmate of Leonard. He'd played banjo in their high-school band, The Buckskin Boys, and had moved into a large wooden house in rural Way's Mill, where Marianne, Axel Joachim and Leonard visited him. Alighting from the bus, which stopped just outside Morton's door, Marianne first witnessed the shocking reds of Canada's maple foliage in autumn.

In Way's Mill, they cooked meals, read poetry aloud and discussed art and politics until late at night. They began work on a film under the direction of Derek May, a Briton who worked for the National Film Board of Canada. Dressing up in lacy dresses and other old clothes yielded by the trunks in Morton's attic, they improvised for the camera. Afterward they went to the river, stripped and swam naked.

Marianne was twenty-seven years old and Leonard twenty-eight. He'd given her a round silver pocket mirror, telling her that never before had a human face given him such joy. She saw *Dr. Zhivago* at the cinema three times and cried no less at the last than at the first. Meanwhile, Leonard and Axel Joachim were home in the bathtub, banging away on the typewriter under water. The experiment ended badly: this was the only occasion the faithful machine broke down in all the years he'd had it. They had dinner in Chinatown and went to Le Bistro on Mountain Street. When they had a babysitter they drank beer and danced at the dancehall. They strolled hand-in-hand down Montreal's Greek street, its small tavernas and bouzouki music reminding them of their days on Hydra.

———

In Montreal there was a constant round of parties, stimulated by drugs and alcohol. The quietude that Leonard needed to write eluded him. The free, pure life under the Greek sun beckoned. When Leonard was awarded a new grant, they finally had the means to go back to Hydra and resume their lives there. It was considerably cheaper to live on a Greek island than in Montreal. Leonard was eager to concentrate on his writing again, and for Marianne life on Hydra was simpler — a social network for herself and her child was already in place.

Chapter 10

FAMILY LIFE ON HYDRA

When Marianne, Axel Joachim and Leonard returned to Hydra it had been a year and a half since they'd last been there. There were still only a few cafés and one bar at the waterfront. The Johnstons and other old acquaintances were there, along with more recently arrived artists and adventurers. Marianne and her son stayed for a short time in the old house in Kala Pigadia, which had been rented during Marianne's absence, bringing her a small income.

Being back in the home she'd shared with Axel felt odd to Marianne. Photographs on the walls, Axel's books, tiny yellow flowers growing on the terrace, the view down to the house where Göran Tundström had lived during his stay on the island — these were all as before. There were still stacks of Axel's novel and short story drafts in the study on the second floor. Marianne didn't disturb the fine layer dust that lay protectively over these relics from the past.

Marianne and Axel Joachim moved in with Leonard. She took the dark brown writing desk that Axel had commissioned from Francisco, the carpenter: now Leonard would write his songs and poems on the smooth Greek tabletop. Marianne also took a wooden fishing winding board that a storm had washed ashore as well as an old carved cradle, a little black table and a handsome chair with a woven seat and carved back. With his eye for small, unusual details, Leonard noticed an old wooden toy train, which he tucked under his arm as they closed the door behind them in Kala Pigadia.

Marianne imparted her womanly touch to Leonard's house. Against the backdrop of a whitewashed wall sat the rattan rocking chair that had rocked the baby to sleep in Kala Pigadia — at two and a half years of age, Axel Joachim was now a big boy who ran around the house. In the entry, they hung the large mirror before which Marianne and Leonard would stand together, considering their reflections. A cross of candle soot marked the main door alcove, where the priest had blessed the house in accordance with local custom when Leonard bought it.

A short time after the little family's return to the island, a letter came from Axel, who was alone in Athens. He'd been banished from the island, he wrote, and he missed his son. Axel thought it was strange and painful that they couldn't see one another, but

. . . don't you think it's best for him if I stay in the
background until he's capable of deciding for himself?
These little guys may ruminate more than one
remembers oneself doing, and in their own way they
take their problems as seriously as we do. Now he's
gotten used to Leonard, that there is a man in the
house, and it doesn't take much fantasy to imagine
the confusion and uncertainty my appearance as
"Pappa" would create for him on top of the travelling,
language difficulties, adjusting to a new place and a
new climate, etc. Since I haven't seen you or heard
anything from you since you got back to Greece I
assume you share my view. How the boy will handle
this situation in the future no one knows. We'll be
damned no matter what we do. I must also get used
to the thought that he will have the sad fate of seeing
his father through his mother's eyes — and in his own

imagination. An impartial picture can't be expected under such circumstances.

By the way, I think you've gotten a good handle on things and by all accounts the boy is thriving and growing and is bright and clever and is no way aggrieved with the world.

As you know, I'm travelling north now. It's as if everything down here has fallen to pieces for me. Maybe it has to do with the fact that one has finally turned thirty, that one sloughs the skin like a snake and wants to move on . . .

I haven't seen anything of Patricia. The capacity of the heart to open and close is peculiar. Like a mussel. Like a tortoise. I feel I can write this to you, like an old friend and confidant with whom I once shared some years of life. . . . Give my regards to Leonard. I have never tried to conceal my admiration of him, and I wish him the very best with the book. The thing about Leonard is that he possesses the secret of getting people to idolize him, and precisely for this reason I will keep myself lurking in the background. It would so very humiliating if I also found myself the victim of his never failing sufferance. Cheers!

Axel[54]

———

Leonard set to work as soon as he was back in the old house. He arose, as usual, at seven in the morning and wrote until lunchtime. Listening to his fingers flying over the keys, Marianne recalled the first time she'd noticed his hands. It had been like looking at the blunt hands of her father. But Leonard typed deftly.

Leonard preferred peace and quiet while he wrote and rarely took his manuscript out of his workroom — in contrast to Axel, who had carried his work with him everywhere. Writing claimed much of Leonard's attention. His inner voice demanded, "Create something! Something beautiful or important or unimportant — just create something!" It had always been that way for him.[55] He didn't share much of what he wrote before it was finished. In any case, Marianne's command of English wasn't good enough to enable her to evaluate what he'd written or even to fully understand it.

KYRIA SOPHIA AND THE SMELL OF HAPPINESS

Not long after they came back they engaged a neighbour, Kyria Sophia, to help around the house. A small woman in her sixties, Sophia didn't even come up to Marianne's shoulders. She wore a grey and white checked housedress and a kerchief bound firmly over her hair. The older woman became like a mother in the house, coming long before they awoke in the morning and looking after them devotedly.

Marianne took care of Axel Joachim and the daily chores while Leonard wrote. At lunchtime Marianne went to the port together with Leonard and the boy, who ran ahead, his body suntanned and his hair as white as chalk. At Katsikas' shop, Marianne filled her shopping basket with vegetables and other provisions. Friends sat outside, around the small lopsided tables. Those with the stomach for it indulged in their first retsina of the day. By one o'clock, after the mail that had come on the boat had been sorted, they all hurried up the steps to the post office, many anxiously crossing their fingers that a cheque would be waiting for them — perhaps from a publisher — to sustain them on Hydra a while longer.

Leonard received cheques from Canada for twelve dollars and fifty cents. Inheriting some stocks from her grandfather, Marianne started getting annual cheques for the equivalent of about two hundred dollars, which allowed them to settle their tab at Katsikas' — they felt like millionaires. Leonard kept their accounts with care, recording in his small notebooks how much they had on credit. They used little money. Marianne sewed her own trousers and wore clothing passed along to her by friends, so there wasn't much she needed to buy. Axel Joachim's clothes were handed down from other children. These garments circulated until nothing was left of them.

When the mail had been collected, everyone went his or her way, uplifted or downcast. Marianne, Axel Joachim and Leonard ascended the steps of the road nicknamed Donkey Shit Lane, through the crossroads known as Four Corners and past a little church until they arrived at the grey-painted wooden door of their house. They shared a meal and then napped through the hottest hours of the day. After the siesta, Leonard closed the door to his study and worked until twilight bathed the house in a blue tinge.

Later they stood in the dusky light before the lovely gold mirror in the hallway and wondered who they were that day. Marianne's round face and sun-bleached hair. Slender and small-breasted. Leonard was about her height, also slim, but black-haired. Neither of them appreciated their own looks. Marianne penned a little poem in her notebook:

> When I know who I am
> I know what to wear
> Till even that becomes
> irrelevant

———

Hydra was arid, with almost no rain from spring until late in the autumn. Marianne and Leonard collected every raindrop in the cistern, as the Hydriots did, using the water in moderation for cooking and washing. Kyria Sophia cleaned the cistern at regular intervals by lowering a bucketful of lime into the water. It hung there a few hours and killed the bacteria.

They purchased their drinking water. Once a week the water man came plodding along with a donkey bearing two great square canisters of water. The old man made his rounds from morning to evening. In exchange for a few coins, he refilled the large ceramic pot — the *kioupi* — that stored drinking water in each household. The little wrinkled, bowlegged man hoisted a container from the donkey's flank and set it on his hip, against a wide leather apron tied around his waist. He carried his heavy load into the house and poured the water into the enormous vessel, which was as high as Marianne's waist.

Kyria Sophia, who had been there since dawn, made a cup of Greek coffee for the old man to drink before he continued on his way. She had already washed the dishes and polished the glass shades of the kerosene lanterns, refilled the lamps and swept the writing room, kitchen and terrace. At ten-thirty in the morning Sophia left Marianne and Leonard and went around the corner to her own house to prepare lunch for her family. Once in a while she would pop in during lunchtime and set a napkin-covered plate of mashed potatoes or *horta* — boiled greens with olive oil and lemon — on their kitchen table.

Life took shape around these routines. Kyria Sophia washed their clothes on the washboard in the marble sink in the basement. Later, she filled the old iron with hot coals and ironed their freshly laundered clothes with even, measured strokes. The smell of chlorine and warm, newly ironed clothes was like the smell of happiness diffusing through the house.[56] Every couple of days, the old woman fetched them ice that came on a caïque from the mainland. Down at the port she tied burlap sacking around the ice block and carried her load up to the house. At home the ice was placed in a wooden crate, from which they tapped cooled water. The clump lasted for two days and cost a couple of drachmas. In the evening Sophia stopped in again to satisfy herself that all was well. The modest monthly salary she received was the equivalent of about fifteen dollars, sufficient to sustain her family.

The stone-walled lanes reverberated with the shouts of Hydriots as they called to one another. Every morning the young nuns, leading four beasts of burden, came down from their high cloister to shop for food. The genial *papas* — priest — strolled by in his grimy old robes that were frayed at the hem. The children teased him and pulled his beard while the adults approached him to kiss his dirty hand.

Waiting for Marianne

I have lost a telephone
with your smell in it
I am living beside the radio
all the stations at once
but I pick out a Polish lullaby
I pick it out of the static
it fades I wait I keep the beat
it comes back almost asleep
did you take the telephone
knowing I'd sniff it immoderately
maybe heat up the plastic
to get all the crumbs of your breath
and if you won't come back
how will you phone to say
you won't come back
so that I could at least argue

Oslo,
May 18, 1962
[Previously unpublished poem by Leonard Cohen][57]

Marianne fell back into her old ways of doing things on Hydra and gradually gained more insights into the local culture. She saw that islanders whipped the old donkeys and mules to get them going but she also observed that they were on the whole well looked after — the animals were their transport and had to be maintained, like a trusty car.

When Marianne and Leonard engaged workmen to put in a new terrace, Marianne offered them home-baked bread and plied them with cold water tinkling with bits of ice to compensate for the sun and heat. Pampered like this, after a while the men hardly bothered to do any work at all. Her old friend George Lialios shook his head at her good-hearted naïveté. "You can't go on like this, Marianne!" he exclaimed. "They're here to fix your terrace and you have to harangue them to get it done. When the job is done, offer them an ouzo." Marianne learned that to survive on the island she had to become more Greek.

In July and August came the strong *meltemi* wind from the north. The warm wind blasted from a cloudless sky for four or five days, dying at sunset and reviving with the rising sun. Under the *meltemi* sailing vessels put vast distances behind them as long as they weren't heading due north. In the autumn came the southerly *sirocco* wind, bearing sandy dust whipped up from the Sahara. Marianne and Leonard secured the doors and windows, but the fine particles crept in everywhere. At their most severe, the sand storms turned the white walls pink. Marianne brushed the sand into a bucket and whitewashed the walls again, as she'd seen the Greek women do. Finally, she swept the stoop outside the house.

In the wintertime the old windows put up a negligible defence against the wind and rain. Marianne and Leonard closed the grey wooden shutters and Kyria Sophia set out a metal tray heaped with glowing coals to warm up the rooms on the first floor. Later they acquired a gas heater, which had wheels and was covered in chicken wire, to warm up the whole house. Marianne often sat in front of the heater, watching the dance of shadows and light while she daydreamed.

"We're going to Bisti on Sunday!" said the women to one another, filling their picnic baskets and rounding up the children. The boatman Mikalis took them along the northern side of Hydra, letting them off at a beautiful secluded beach just short of the island's western tip, from where the island of Spetses could be seen. They made themselves comfortable with cushions and blankets. The children played on the beach while the adults slaked their thirst with cold beer and retsina. They swam and ate and took siesta in the shade of the pine trees.

Mikalis was accompanied by his son, who leaped overboard with the rope to fasten the boat when they approached land. The boatman smiled with pride. When the son grew up, he followed in his father's footsteps and became a seaman. But as fate would have it, one day the young man was entangled in an anchor line and drowned. Mikalis became a shadow of himself and never recovered. Years later, Marianne and Leonard would hear him singing sorrowfully as he staggered home from the port late in the evenings. They stopped for a moment to listen as his dirges melted into the night.

———

More and more foreigners had come to Hydra during the four years that had elapsed since Marianne and Axel first stepped onto the port. Artists interested in the simple life came from New York and other cities. A married couple had ambitions of farming organically on Hydra, but soon discovered that the stony soil was barely cultivable. Marianne met a Russian prince who lived in London and who gave her his visiting card: "Prince" it stated. People like the Johnstons and George Lialios had settled on the island for the long term, but most were there for shorter periods before going on to explore other destinations.

Among the longest resident expatriates, the Johnstons were a natural social hub for the foreigners who gathered at the waterfront when the sun went down. There were rousing conversations, wild dancing and drunkenness as couples cleaved and hived off with new partners. The uninhibited expatriates were tolerated by the native islanders and provided a kind of live entertainment for them.

George and Charmian drank heavily and often had to be carried home. Leonard and his Greek friend Demetri Gassoumis would go down to the port to check if George and Charmian were fit to return home on their own feet. The Johnstons' marital problems were exacerbated when George was diagnosed with tuberculosis of the lungs. Beautiful and talented, Charmian desired the attention of men, while her husband was sick and impotent. The English painter Anthony Kingsmill was immediately smitten with Charmian when he first laid eyes on the dark-haired beauty, whom he asked to model for him. Their love affair was an open secret, with George relegated to the role of the jealous husband. New affairs and fresh threats of divorce were continual — Marianne and Leonard couldn't keep count of the quarrels they'd involuntarily witnessed.

Living on the island was like being under a loupe: all goings-on were exaggerated and there was no place to hide from public view. A love affair became common knowledge and everyone was dragged into it. If someone drank too much, his alcoholic dissolution was observed by everyone.

———

Morning and evening, the landscape was enveloped in a warm light that infused Marianne with serenity. Loose dogs barked in the back streets. Neighbours whispered in the dark on their terraces. A woman shifted some potted plants in her garden. From the window Marianne could see red roof tiles and blue, green and purple woodwork. Pink blooms spilling over white walls. She heard the church bells ringing. She slept next to Leonard under a mosquito net. Made love under the same white net. Wrote in her blue-lined notebook that "it's good to be naked in one's own house." By the light of an oil lamp, Leonard read poems to her on the terrace. Not sure what was a dream and what was real, Marianne could only be certain this was her life and that this was where she wanted to be. Here, now.

FREE UNDER THE SUN

Before the expatriates arrived with their alien sexual attitudes, it was unheard of among Hydriots for young men and women to be lovers before they were married. Marianne had on many occasions seen a blood-spotted white sheet hung out so that everyone could see that the bride had been a virgin on her wedding night. It was common for girls to walk hand in hand and for boys to do the same, and for Greek youths their first sexual experience was often with the same sex. Homosexuality had ancient roots in Greece, where during antiquity certain forms of the practice were widespread and socially approved.[58]

In the 1960s, homosexuals from different parts of the world sought out Greece, where they could live out their sexual orientations. Some came to Hydra as couples, while others arrived singly, establishing sexual relationships with the young Greeks they met on the island. It was not unusual to see foreign men accompanied by Greek youths, and as far as Marianne could tell this did not seem to be a matter of controversy among the islanders.

Marianne and Leonard were close friends with the American couple Chuck Hulse and Gordon Merrick. The two young men were inseparable. Axel Joachim called them "ChuckandGordon," regardless of whether he was referring to Chuck or Gordon: for him they were one and the same person. Gordon wrote novels with homosexuality as the theme and had enjoyed great success with his debut *The Strumpet Wind*, which came out in 1947. The book contained autobiographical elements and concerned a gay

American spy in France during the Second World War.

Marianne and Leonard kept some thriving marijuana plants near the outhouse in their yard. Greece had been an important producer of hemp — used for making rope and textiles — since the middle of the nineteenth century. The use of hashish was pronounced in the shipping towns and was associated with rembetiko, a form of Greek folk music. The music of the working class, rembetiko originated in the early 1900s, a time of political chaos and widespread unemployment and poverty. Especially in the checkered milieu of Piraeus, men repaired to hash dens to listen to music and escape from reality.[59] Growing marijuana was widespread in Greece, and up until the military seized power in 1967 the police often looked the other way at the use of the plant as a narcotic.

Once in a while Marianne cut up some marijuana leaves and kneaded them into her meatball mix along with grated onions. Everyone was happy to be invited to dinner when Marianne's meatballs were on the menu.

One day when Kyria Sophia's daughter was there, she pointed at the pot plants and said sternly, "Very dangerous!" Marianne and Leonard hid the plants among some other flowers in the garden and let them remain there, for domestic use. Some years later Marianne read in the paper that the farmers of Crete were no longer allowed to cultivate marijuana. She and Leonard uprooted the few plants they still had growing in the garden, dried them and called it "oregano."

––––––

The foreign women on Hydra helped one another with childcare. Many had small children but not all had babysitters. If there was a marital problem at one household the children could spend a night or two at a friend's house until things had settled down. Flower-power people took their children with them everywhere but Marianne, sticking to Norwegian tradition, wanted her son to be in bed when evening came. Without electricity the house was dark, and she didn't dare to have the oil lamps on when she and Leonard were out in case one should be overturned. If he awoke, Axel Joachim could call from the terrace to the neighbour girl, Sophia: "*Ella Sophia* — Come, Sophia!" But Marianne preferred to have a babysitter in the house.

The gang of girlfriends frequently gathered in Marianne's kitchen to prepare dishes originating in places like China or other Asian regions. For many, Hydra was a stop between Europe and India, and an Eastern inspiration was reflected in the foods they made. The women would bring diverse ingredients and spend the whole day cooking. Chocolate mousse spiked with marijuana was the specialty of Olivia de Haulleville, who had grown up in the home of her uncle, Aldous Huxley. Olivia was married to Georgos Kassipidis, a Greek, and they had a daughter who was Axel Joachim's age.

One day a package came from India. A friend of Georgos had sent home a toy mule — named Jack — and everyone swarmed to Georgos and Olivia's house. Full of anticipation, they gathered around Georgos while he cracked open Jack's belly. Inside lay a big lump of hashish, which was waxed to prevent the telltale aroma from leaking out. They carved off a little and smoked it in a pipe while giving thanks to Tibet. Marianne floated, feeling that all her senses had been opened.

Marianne had the impression of entering a temple when she stepped through the doorway of Olivia's house, resplendent with colourful Indian rugs and cushions that dazzled the eyes. Olivia played oriental music and introduced Marianne to Buddhism. They lived near each other and once in a while Olivia slept over, sharing Marianne's bed. One morning Marianne awoke to find a little poem on the pillow, addressed "To my darling Nordic troll." On another occasion Olivia disappeared over the mountain without warning. Georgos looked after their child while his wife was on her jaunt; she returned two days later. In comparison to her exotic and adventurous friend, Marianne felt like a staid country bumpkin.

Olivia and Georgos's daughter slept on the floor below the main level of the house. Marianne couldn't help smiling to herself as she observed Olivia close the hatch in the kitchen floor after the little girl had gone to sleep — it was as if the child had been tidied away for the evening.

MOTHER-IN-LAW'S VISIT

The summer that Leonard's mother came to visit him, Marianne vacated the house to avoid offending her religious sensibilities. Just a few days into Masha's stay, Leonard implored Marianne to move back in. His mother was complaining about the heat, Leonard couldn't write and the visit was turning into a catastrophe. Marianne took Axel Joachim back to the house and they all spent a week together under the same roof. Leonard's mother went into fits of pique just about every other day: it was too warm or too cold, or something else wasn't right. She packed her suitcases and a donkey was sent for, to carry her things down to the port. Moments later she would have a change of heart and decide to stay.

In spite of her capriciousness and excitability, Marianne became good friends with her "mother-in-law." Masha had taken to Axel Joachim. Playing with him and feeding him, she became another person when she was near the child. The sight of the two of them together warmed Marianne. It was as if the boy had gained an extra grandmother. Leonard thanked Marianne and, with a little smile, said that he would have killed his mother had it not been for her.

Marianne and her little boy communicated in Norwegian. Leonard said it was wonderful to hear this foreign language and to be admitted into the world of this white-haired child who came from the land of snow and who spoke a tongue he couldn't understand.

She was often nervous that the boy would bother Leonard while he was working but Leonard claimed the child was possibly what he loved most about her. He could calm Axel Joachim and get him to bed when Marianne couldn't manage it. When Leonard heard her arguing with the child in the kitchen he would gallantly open the door to his workroom and say, "Axel, I need your help." Before long, Axel Joachim lay quietly under the desk, drawing, while Leonard continued with his work. The boy enjoyed being with Leonard, whom he simply called "Cone."

After Marianne had tucked Axel Joachim into bed in the evening she couldn't relax completely, anxious that the child might wake up during their love-making or other private moments she and Leonard shared. And it troubled Marianne that Axel Joachim wasn't Leonard's child and that they shared a home without being husband and wife. Leonard asked her many times if she found their way of living problematic; she lied and assured him that everything was fine.

TO PARIS

Nightmares sometimes cast a shadow over Marianne's days — she couldn't shake her unease about the future and the fate of her relationship with Leonard. He couldn't make any promises to her and didn't want to get married. Marianne didn't believe marriage was the solution for them, but she was also afraid that, once again, she would be left on her own. Another concern for her was that having a child rendered her less free to follow Leonard on his travels. From the outside it all looked so perfect. There were good meals and flowers on the table, but her face was often drawn with sadness. When Leonard asked what was wrong, she answered, "Nothing, nothing's wrong." She wasn't able to express her fears and neither was she content with what Leonard was able to give her. The sense that they were living together on borrowed time gnawed at her.

The first draft of Leonard's first novel, *The Favourite Game*, had been turned down by McClelland & Stewart. Since their return to Hydra he'd been working on the revision and he planned to go the States late in the autumn of 1962 to wrap up the book. The semi-autobiographical novel concerned a young man in Montreal who pursued his calling as a poet.

In addition to closing the book deal, it was important for Leonard to renew his connection with the metropolis. Hydra's primitive, pared-down conditions fostered the inner tranquility and discipline that he needed to write, but he also required recharging from another kind of environment and other stimuli. In the same way he could feel impeded by Montreal, extended stays on Hydra made him feel stagnant.[60] Moreover, he calculated that he and Marianne required as little as eleven hundred dollars per year to sustain them on Hydra. On the other side of the Atlantic, he could earn enough money for another year in Greece.

Leonard was frustrated that he couldn't live off his writing, despite the rave reviews his work had received. He didn't know what to do — the only things he was good at were writing and playing the guitar. Marianne noticed that Leonard was becoming restless. He asked her what she wanted to do most — if she wanted to stay on Hydra or if she desired something else. Again, she found herself unable to say what she truly wanted, which was to be wherever he was. Instead, she told him that it had crossed her mind to go to Paris to learn French and to model. She'd served as a model for painters and photographers on Hydra and had been encouraged to try to model professionally.

The thought that she and Axel Joachim would be left alone on Hydra while Leonard was in the U.S. made Marianne disconsolate, so she made up her mind to go to Paris. However, she didn't think it was a good idea to take her son — not quite three years old — to a new big city, where they had no one to support them. Marianne asked her mother to look after him in Oslo while she was in France.

Marianne wrote to Axel, from whom she hadn't heard in a long time, to apprise him of her plans. He was living with Lena Folke-Olsson and their firstborn child in a house owned by his publisher near Larvik, on the western shore of the Oslo Fjord. On the 15th of November she received his reply, which explained that he was screwing up the nerve to write some sort of masterpiece or other and that he was fed up with roaming the crust of the earth, leading a "poetic" lifestyle. Axel also informed her that he was prepared to take on full responsibility for his son if Marianne was willing to agree to his terms.

> Dear Marianne, Len and Little Axel,
>   So now you're thinking of learning French, Little Axel is going to his granny and Leonard to the States. That's the way it is and there's little I can say about it. Naturally, my resignation is mixed with a good portion of concern about the boy. We would be more than happy to have him here, but the place is remote and it would be quite dreary and lonely for him here after life on Hydra. That we have peace and quiet here wouldn't carry much weight with a child, but I think that the contrast would get him thinking and missing you and his playmates on Hydra. If there were more hustle and bustle here he would tire himself out and not have time to turn inward and sulk. I'm also worried about the inner chain reaction that a parent switch like this could trigger in anyone. Don't think this has anything to do with unwillingness on my part. I'm just trying to do what's best for him (as we parents are fond of saying). At the risk of wounding and offending you, may I propose another suggestion (which you will reject even before you reach the end of the sentence) and that is that we keep the boy for an undetermined period of time and you cannot make

any demands on him until you are able to offer him a settled, harmonious situation. If you absolutely must go to Paris to learn French (and may God go with you) I agree that that it's hardly the ideal place to drag a little tot. That he stays with his grandmother is certainly a good choice but, as I said, my suggestion is open and you think it through the best you can. . . .

Give Leonard my regards and my wishes for all the luck in life, the gods know if we'll ever see each another again. My exit from Hydra was an unfortunate affair that drained me and seems to have thrown me on the rocks of defeat.[61]

Marianne is lonely without Leonard, who is in the U.S. for an indefinite period of time. It's not the same when it's just her and Axel Joachim in the house, and the days drag by slowly. She exchanges telegrams and a few letters with Leonard; otherwise her thoughts and longings end up in her diary.

The weeks pass. Mother and child follow their daily routines. In the evenings, Marianne sits in the deep windowsill on the second floor, her eyes resting on the horizon. It's the only spot in the house with a view of the sea and when the moon shines its borrowed light, millions of crystals glitter on the water's surface. Axel Joachim sleeps under his mosquito net on the first floor. The hens in Evgania's backyard have settled down for the night. During the day the chickens produce an incessant cheerful racket. When Leonard is home they sometimes aim peas at them just for the fun of seeing the comical birds burst into action.

Some evenings Marianne walks to the old cemetery and sits among the gravestones, the black-and-white photographs and icons and oil lamps. She is not afraid. The moon and the little oil lamps provide all the light she needs. Time seems to stand still. Sitting there until dawn and treasuring the tranquility that dissipates with daybreak, Marianne inhabits — as Momo had tried to teach her — a place inside herself.

By not asking to accompany him, Marianne has granted Leonard the freedom she knows he desires. But it has cost her dearly. The only way to achieve a balance is to create something with her own life and her own experiences. She weighs again the pros and cons of going to Paris or staying on Hydra. In any case, she will not accept Axel's offer. After a few months on Hydra she resolves to follow through with her plan to go Paris: she needs to get away. Her son will be well looked after by his grandmother in Oslo. It won't be for long anyway: she wasn't thinking of an extended stay in France. If she ends up prolonging her time there, she'll make arrangements for Axel Joachim to join her.

———

In Paris Marianne stayed with a friend of Leonard, Madeleine Lerch, who was a model and could help her with contacts. Madeleine was the girlfriend of the director Derek May, whom Marianne had met when they lived in Montreal and made the film at Morton Rosengarten's house in Way's Mills. Madeleine's apartment lay on Rue de Savoie, in an exclusive part of the sixth arrondissement, by the Seine. Moving into the sleeping alcove in the living room, Madeleine relinquished the only bedroom to Marianne. Madeleine was dark and beautiful, Marianne blond and Nordic. It didn't take long before the first meeting with a photographer was arranged.

Nervously, Marianne walked up to the big atelier. She wore a black dress with silk lining and a zipper up the back that her mother had sewn for her when she had hoped her daughter was going to take up secretarial work in Oslo. Not speaking a word of French, Marianne received instructions in broken English and posed to the best of her ability as the photographer shot a strip of photographs of her, seated on the floor in the clean lines of her classic dress. Afterward he invited her out to dinner. During the meal he asked if she would go to bed with him. Marianne declined.

That was the last she heard from the French photographer. The only thing she was left with was a strip of small black-and-white pictures. She had no income, and having Axel Joachim living at her mother's in Oslo was only a stopgap. Leonard had his calling and was devoted to his work, while Marianne felt steadily more seized up when it came to finding her way. Up to now she'd gone wherever love led her.

Her financial circumstances were becoming increasingly straitened. She had some dividends from the stocks inherited from her grandfather but it wasn't enough to make ends meet in a city like Paris. She was considering sending Axel Joachim to private school, as was common in France and among their coterie on Hydra. He would benefit from a good education and a more structured life, and she would have more freedom. With this in mind, Marianne decided to try to extract from Axel the child support she was entitled to, so she wrote to him and explained the situation.

Not long afterward a letter tumbled through the mail slot on Rue de Savoie:

Dear Marianne,

Sooner or later there had to come a letter from your hand. And that the letter comes a hair's breadth from the point that you characterize as "down to the last cent" doesn't confuse me. Now, no bad memories. Just this: The money for Axel Joachim has not in any way been forgotten but has been taken good care of. It's hopeless to discuss this via letters, but it disappoints me not a little that I have not heard a word from you about how the boy is doing, yes, it makes me so furious that I decided to put the money into a special account until I got a sign of life from you.

Now I've received a sign of life. You are in Paris. You want to put Little Axel in a private school. It's impossible for me to take a position on this on the spot, but the 200 kroner we've agreed to for the boy still stands, of course.[62]

For a month Marianne trod the broad wooden steps that wound elegantly up to Madeleine's apartment in the Latin Quarter. She missed Axel Joachim, she missed Leonard. Through the high narrow windows in the living room she looked over at the neighbour's and beyond to the Seine, flowing at its stately pace. But she was unable enjoy Paris and she couldn't think about attempting a new modelling assignment after that initial debacle. Without a grasp of French, it would be almost futile for her to seek other kinds of employment.

———

The October wind rustled in the trees along the river and the colourful leaves danced weightlessly down to the sidewalks. Marianne had been wandering around Paris for hours. The old ring she habitually wore had been irritating her all day. When she was together with Axel she'd inherited a piece of jewellery with an oval golden-yellow topaz from her father's mother. Marianne had Axel's cousin, who was a goldsmith, turn the old-fashioned piece into a large ring for her. She wore it often, but for some reason that day it was just a bother. She twisted the ring around her finger until she couldn't stand it any more and took it off and put it in her bag.

In the evening, her mother called from Oslo to break the news that Marianne's father's mother had been hit by a car and had died.

Marianne had tried in vain to find a path toward self-realization in Paris. It was time to go home to Axel Joachim.

Chapter 11

LONGING AND JEALOUSY

When Marianne was away from Hydra, Leonard sent cables. "Will you come to Greece now? Love Leonard." His letters said that it was strange to be on the island without her and to discover how much of the island was Marianne and how much was just stone and sun.

While Marianne was in Norway for the funeral of her paternal grandmother, Leonard, who had been in London and Canada for several months, wrote that he was on his way back to Greece. He missed Marianne and their blind love in which sun-browned bodies spoke their wordless language.[63]

Leonard reckoned he'd been poorly paid for the novel that he'd spent two years writing, and wanted to go back to Hydra. He sent a complaining letter to a friend in Canada. London depressed him, he said. He was going to Hydra to be with a Norwegian woman and her child — he would "become a husband and father in one fell swoop."[64] He couldn't afford to live anywhere else than Hydra, he said, yet being on the island isolated him from his cultural background and modern currents.

———

Marianne loved living on Hydra. She was at home there and felt she was at her best there. In Oslo, without a social network, she was adrift. She knew everyone on Hydra and after all these years she felt almost like an Hydriot. She enjoyed looking after the home she and Leonard had together brought into being and she seldom felt lonely. During a cold, dark winter evening she might long to be away from the island, but the rhythm she had established for herself on Hydra gave her pleasure and satisfaction. When Leonard rejoined her on the island, there was no other place else she wished to be. Hydra was their paradise.

They lived as a family again, Leonard the bread-winner, Marianne the mother and housewife, muse and lover. As before, Leonard sat writing in his study or on the terrace, Ray Charles on the portable record player beside him. In the mornings Marianne set a fresh gardenia on his work desk. In the evenings Leonard read poems to her. Marianne nurtured his writing and maintained the structure within which he worked well. There was order and harmony in the house. Leonard later said that it wasn't just that Marianne was his muse who shined before him; she also realized that it was important to get him to sit down and write.[65]

Marianne often went swimming with the other women and their children. Axel Joachim was nearly four years of age and spoke Greek, English and Norwegian. During the day he scampered from house to house and played with the other children. When they had visitors in the evening, the little boy leaned out of his second-floor window and listened in on the incomprehensible conversations the adults were carrying on below. When Marianne and Leonard were out, Axel Joachim could call to the babysitter, young Sophia, from his bedroom window. Sometimes he took his plastic potty and announced he was going to spend the night at the neighbours', where they slept several to a bed.

Marianne and Leonard had gradually created a home together. The view wasn't grand, by the standards of Hydra, but the large L-shaped house was beautiful. Its numerous small rooms were appointed with furnishings passed on to them by friends. When people were flush they upgraded their furniture and kitchen equipment, as the Johnstons had done before giving Leonard their old kitchen table. Beside the ornate Russian wrought iron bed that Leonard had bought, their bookcase gradually filled with books. Axel Joachim was allowed to draw on the whitewashed walls in his room. His imagination given free reign, Axel Joachim delineated long roads that meandered over the uneven surfaces of the stone walls.

Not a wall in the house was straight. Minute crystals in the lime wash caught the sunlight and reflected back a soft lustre completely different than ordinary paint. When evening fell and the oil lamps were lit, the luminous whitewash made everyone look beautiful.[66]

Leonard had a knack for nosing out beautiful objects. When he'd been apart from Marianne, he always returned to her bearing small gifts. A pair sewing scissors in the form of a little bird that sliced with its beak. An Yves Saint Laurent pocket mirror edged with tortoiseshell.

Before the old mirror where Leonard and Marianne would stand and behold themselves was a small table crowded with gifts from visitors along with small prizes they'd found themselves: a piece of driftwood, a bit of coloured beach glass, an old iron. "Oh, that's the most beautiful thing I've ever seen," a guest would say, holding up one of the treasures. "It's yours," Marianne or Leonard typically responded.

New film teams and artists were constantly arriving. Melina Mercouri and her French director husband Jules Dassin filmed scenes for *Phaedra* in the bay where Marianne and Leonard regularly swam. Mercouri was a big star in Greece, where she was famous as an actress and a singer, and had attained international celebrity with the film *Never on Sunday*. She would later become Greece's Minister for Culture.

As Leonard became more widely known, the flow of visitors who came knocking on their door swelled. Marianne played her part as the hostess, while Leonard grew frustrated with the interruptions. They began to withdraw from the social scene at the port. In any case, Marianne couldn't go out in the evenings without having arranged for a sitter for Axel Joachim. Sometimes Leonard took off on his own. In Marianne's eyes, Leonard emanated a kind of light that attracted people who came near him. She was keenly aware of the pull that women felt toward him.

———

Marianne continued modelling for the artists on Hydra. The French–Canadian painter Marcelle Maltais painted a portrait of Marianne and Axel Joachim that now belongs to the National Museum of Fine Arts in Quebec. Anthony Kingsmill painted her in his tiny home, which comprised a kitchen and another room on the first floor and, reached by narrow stairs, the single room on the second storey that served as his atelier. Marianne posed nude on a cushion as sand drizzled down on her head from the old sticks and plaster ceiling. Anthony affixed a sheet of paper to his easel, walked right up to Marianne, took some sight measurements with his pencil, retreated to the far end of the room and did a few little dance steps before advancing to his easel and finally putting pencil to paper. Thus he paced forth and back, executing his dainty footwork, as his sketch made slow but sure progress.

Anthony didn't have two pennies to rub together. The artist survived on advance payments for paintings that were often never completed. He gambled or drank the money away. The painting of Marianne was lost in a poker game. Leonard bought several of his friend's pieces — some he received, some he didn't.

Life on the island had become intractable for many. George Johnston, unwell and thin as a rail, still held court at the table at Katsikas', where everyone bore witness to the intensifying rancour between him and his wife. When George and Charmian were drunk they aired all their dirty laundry and set about wounding each other viciously, mainly with words but on the worst occasions they ended up in physical scrimmages. Marianne was pained watching her friends ruin each other and themselves.

Another marriage to suffer was that between Marianne's friend Magda and her husband, the proprietors of Lagoudera. Magda's husband met an Egyptian princess at the Hilton Hotel in Athens and ran off with her. He'd landed in trouble with the police and since he was now out of the reach of the law Magda took the punishment. She was sent to a women's prison in Athens. When she was released several months later her vibrant red hair had gone grey. Lagoudera's inventory had been auctioned off; everything Magda had built up was gone.

Marianne saw Magda almost daily after she got out of prison. One day as the two women lay sunning themselves on the big flat rocks by the sea, a figure appeared at the top of the cliff, above them. The man stood there a while before he dived into the sea with the grace of a swallow. After first displaying himself to Magda in this way, the sailor Theodores kept showing up wherever she was. The pair were eventually married and were devoted to each other for many years. Magda — Marianne's Czech "big sister" — died in the old-age home on Hydra in the autumn of 2005.

VISIT TO NORWAY

When Marianne left for Oslo to visit her family again, Leonard, who'd been in Montreal, followed her. Marianne had borrowed the apartment of a friend who'd fallen in love with a man on Hydra and was staying there a while. The elegant apartment in the western part of Oslo was at her disposal for a couple of months. As soon as Leonard arrived, he jumped into the bathtub to rid himself of the lice he'd picked during the trans-Atlantic passage he'd scrounged on a freighter. There he lay, at regular intervals, applying creams and potions in a desperate attempt to destroy the little beasts.

They went to the Theatre Café and ate *lutefisk* — dried cod treated with lye and served boiled. Leonard saw Ibsen's work performed at the National Theatre and they visited family and friends. In the seventh floor apartment, Leonard took in the view over Oslo, listened to the radio and danced by himself when Marianne was out and he couldn't concentrate on the book he was working on. The scale of Oslo, the buildings and the snow, reminded him of Montreal. Watching Marianne as she leaned out of the window to issue motherly warnings to Axel Joachim, Leonard learned the expression *Ikke lek i gaten* — Don't play in the street.

During his stay in Oslo, Leonard wrote to his old friend Irving Layton, in Canada, that Marianne

> . . . seems to have endured and ruined the women I've
> known after her and I've got to confront her mystery
> in the snow. She is so blonde in my heart! . . .
> I've been working on my new book but today feel
> like giving up writing. The air is too sweet for all this
> working of the mind, the herrings are too tasty. When
> I am not watching blonde girls I am eating herring
> and sometimes I do both.[67]

———

Back on Hydra, Leonard embarked on his second novel, *Beautiful Losers*, in 1964 and entered an intense period of writing. He wrote with great concentration out on the terrace, breaking only for lunch and a siesta in the middle of the day. He described it as an ideal time to set to work:

> There was a woman, she had a child, there were
> meals on the table, order in the upkeep of the house
> and harmony. It was the perfect moment to start to
> do some serious work . . . When there is food on the
> table, when the candles are lit, when you wash the
> dishes together and put the child to bed together.

That is order, that is spiritual order, there is no other.[68]

The new book revolved around the figure of the Native American saint, Kateri Tekákwitha,[69] also known as Lily of the Mohawks, with whom Leonard was deeply fascinated. Leonard told Marianne that he lay flowers at the little statue of Kateri in Saint Patrick's Cathedral when he was in New York. Marianne had always loved to listen to stories like these, dreaming herself away as she had done as a girl, reading under the eiderdown or listening to her grandmother's fairy tales. Leonard usually said little about his work, but he read his poetry to her and he played his guitar for her as they sat alone on the terrace.

JEALOUSY

Leonard often had a need to socialize after a long day at the typewriter, whereas Marianne was housebound until the babysitter came. When he went to the port before she did, she invariably found a beautiful woman sitting beside him when she came down to join him. Marianne was stabbed by jealousy. She observed the dissolution of the relationships around them and was conscious of the fragility of what she and Leonard shared. Hydra nourished art but not marriage, and many came seeking romantic adventures — as she had done.

Marianne often found herself wishing that she could erect a cage around Leonard so she could swallow the key and keep him all to herself. Leonard was attentive, a gentleman with an eye for women. They loved the appreciative way he looked at them and trailed after him. The knowledge that he was living with *her* — had chosen *her* — should have kept Marianne's head high, but she couldn't help feeling small and insecure every time she saw women flocking around him.

When a beautiful young American came to Hydra, Leonard

disappeared for an entire day as the two of them went up the mountain together. Everything imaginable flooded Marianne's mind. She curled up in a ball on the floor and thought that she wanted to die, while she constructed an imaginary coffin around herself. People who came in assumed she was sleeping and stole out again. She lay like that all day, without communicating with anyone, engulfed by her own morbid fantasy, which was as vivid as any of her girldhood daydreams. She awoke the next morning and regarded her own deadened gaze in the mirror. But Leonard had come home and she could breathe again.

_____

Leonard left more often, crossing the Atlantic to add to his bank account and to accrue inspiration for his work. Fewer ideas came to him on Hydra and travelling stimulated him. His collection of poems *Flowers for Hitler* came out in 1964. Leonard dedicated the book "To Marianne."

Now in great demand in Canada, Leonard steadily received invitations to read his poetry around the country. The directors Donald Brittain and Don Owen began work on their documentary *Ladies and Gentlemen, Mr. Leonard Cohen*. Filming took place during poetry readings in Montreal and at the house on Hydra, where the camera zoomed in on the strip of little black and white photographs of Marianne in Paris that hung by the writing desk in Leonard's sparsely furnished study.

Marianne waited in the whitewashed house while Leonard boosted his life and his writing elsewhere in Europe and in North America. She found it harder to be alone on Hydra while Leonard was away. They seldom had the means for both of them to travel, and besides, travelling was something Leonard preferred to do on his own. Difficulties that were easily resolved when they were together became impenetrable when an ocean lay between them. Their relationship began to crack as the external pressures mounted.

Leonard: Our relationship was not secure. She'd go back to Norway, I to Canada to try to make some money. We were young, and both of us interested in all kinds of experience, so there was something fragile about the relationship. I was hungry for experience as any young writer is, and every young person. I wanted many women, many kinds of experiences, many countries, many climates, many love affairs. I didn't know it at the time, but it was natural for me then to see life as some kind of buffet where there was a lot of different tastes. I'd get tired of something and then move on to something else, never terribly happy doing it, leaving one thing for the next because the thing I had didn't work, whether it was the woman or the poem or the city or whatever it was — it wasn't working. Until I understood that nothing works. But that took me a lifetime to understand that nothing works and to accept that.[70]

I have a sense that I was privileged. The sunlight, the woman, the child, the table, the work, the gardenia, the order, the mutual respect and honour that we gave to each other. That's what really matters. I know there were all kinds of problems. We were kids, and we lived in a period during which the old forms were overthrown. We wanted to overthrow the forms that had been given to us but at the same time maintain things that seemed to be nourishing.[71]

Those relationships on Hydra were all doomed. We didn't know it at the time, but they couldn't withstand what life imposed on us. Those relationships that were formed idealistically or sexually or romantically couldn't survive the challenges that ordinary lives would confront them with. None of those relationships survived, except in the sense that we honour them and we recognize the nourishment of those experiences.[72]

Chapter 12

A STATION ON THE WAY

Perpetually beset by self-doubt, Marianne had never placed her complete faith in anyone around her either, with the exception of her grandmother. She had told Momo everything, knowing that her confidences would never be used against her. Even to Leonard she couldn't bare her feelings. Instead, Marianne made it easy for him to leave her and easy for him to come back. Talking to Leonard inside her head, Marianne wrote in English in her diary:

> God, help me get it together. I'm reading and reading
> — everything from Jung to old letters from Leonard
> and my own notes from years ago. So where am I? Still
> empty and confused and sort of dead inside. I don't go
> out. I need to be alone. I have little to give to others. I
> have to dig deep down to find my own soul. If I find it,
> maybe I could be of some use to the people around me.
> My head is empty, and I'm tired of doing nothing.
> In a way I wish I could break away from everything, go
> somewhere and change everything. Live differently.
> Leave this island once and for all. I've been here long
> enough. It's all over, Baby Blue.

In the spring of 1965 Marianne and Axel Joachim accompanied Leonard to London. She didn't like being left on Hydra every time he went away, and this time they could afford for the three of them to make the trip. As fate, or irony, would have it, Leonard ran into Lena Folke-Olsson — Axel's girlfriend — in Oxford Street. Marianne soon received a letter from Axel:

So I heard that you were in London too. But since there are at least five thousand reasons why you didn't make an effort to meet me I won't bother you with that. I'm writing for three reasons:

1/ — Georg Johannesen (in my humble opinion our most significant lyric poet, even though he chisels in stone more than he fingers his lyre) has sent me an SOS from Budapest where he's staying with his Jewish girlfriend for the time being. He asks if "my" house can be rented (quote) "in the summer and through the autumn, or from August and through the winter." Is there anyone living there? he asks. It's not my house, so now I'm asking you . . .

2/ — In her zeal to secure a monthly child support payment for Little Axel your mother has found it necessary to go to the Oslo bailiff's office, which is sending its threat letters to the consulate here in London, ensuring that the name Axel Jensen leaves behind a nice trail for all eternity for the benefit of future literature professors and biographers. Our son will have something to be ashamed of, reading about "Axel Jensen the Evil" in literary history. Quite frankly, I must say that it's a shame that it was deemed necessary to go the way of the Philistines. I ought to hire myself a lawyer (if I could afford one) to handle the correspondence between us . . . Be that as it may, I have no money now and I don't count on getting any until the manuscript is ready at Cappelen.

What now. Yes, point three. There was a point

three. But now I've forgotten what point three was. It must have been something pleasant because otherwise I wouldn't have forgotten it.

Right, now I remember! Are you well? That was point three. Are you well?

Perhaps that should have been point one. But it ended being point three instead.[73]

After a short stay in London the little family returned together to Hydra. Decompressing from his deep immersion in his work on *Beautiful Losers*, Leonard broke down when he finally completed the novel. He came down with a fever, hallucinated and lost weight rapidly. Marianne found it difficult to connect with him.

When their housekeeper Kyria Sophia came in and saw that all was not as it should be, she took Marianne in her embrace, stroking her and speaking soothingly to her in Greek. Marianne's Greek was poor, but to Sophia — who was in many ways like her grandmother — she didn't need to say anything. Kyria Sophia often ordered Marianne and Leonard to sit down to eat something or other she'd prepared for them. The old woman made nettle soup, and the wild greens and herbs that she harvested from the hills and the shore she boiled and served splashed with olive oil. When her husband fell ill Sophia made him a tea from a plant that grew on stones in the sea. Her son-in-law took her out in his little fishing boat. She folded up her sleeves and hung over the edge of the boat as she gathered the seaweed in a big sack. Her husband drank the infusion she brewed and recovered.

———

People arrived and departed, but Marianne remained on Hydra. She kept the house in order and the walls white and clean. There were plenty of opportunities for excursions and diversions but she didn't take advantage of them. Leonard cabled eagerly when he was away. "How are you little lost friend?" "We're getting through on all levels." "Don't go to China without me. See you soon. Leonard."

Many travelled between Hydra and the East, where they tried to find themselves through experiments with narcotics and meditation. Olivia, Marianne's neighbour and friend, went to India. Zina Rachevsky, rumoured to be a Russian princess, came to Hydra from New York together with her son Alexander. She had dedicated her life to Buddhism and was on her way to Nepal to become a nun. As before, a steady stream of writers, painters and filmmakers came and went.

More and more people came to find Leonard, but he shied away from this kind of attention. "I have to make myself invisible tonight," he told Marianne, before going down to the port in the evening. Leonard didn't drink much when he was out, though he was partial to Norwegian line aquavit. Marianne didn't need more than a glass of retsina to loosen up. With a little alcohol in her bloodstream her fear of fluffing her English slackened and she spoke more freely.

Language often snarled up their relationship. Years earlier, Leonard had looked at Axel's dusty typewriter and noticed its peculiar Norwegian characters, like å and ø, which barred him from their world. To Leonard, the letters in Axel's drawers resembled his own yet they were alien to him. He couldn't understand what Marianne said to her child in Norwegian, and she didn't grasp the nuances of the English language. The resulting misunderstandings could lead to quarrels. Leonard might ask her if she would help him with something, to which Marianne would reply, "I can manage." To Leonard's ears, this hinted that it would take a sizeable effort to oblige him and she wasn't enthusiastic about it. But what Marianne had meant was that it would be no trouble to fulfil his request and she would gladly do it. They were best when they weren't talking about themselves and were instead focused on carrying out their daily tasks.

GLOBE-TROTTING

Leonard's career as a singer began in 1966, when he was forced to concede that he couldn't make a living as a writer. *Beautiful Losers* had received good reviews but sold marginally. Once, with a smile, he'd admitted to Marianne that he fantasized about making a song that got into jukeboxes.

Leonard had been away from Hydra a great deal during the last couple of years, and matters between him and Marianne were troubled. In an effort to pull their relationship back together, they decided to go back to Montreal and establish a new base for themselves there. They moved into a modest apartment at 3657 Aylmer Street. Axel Joachim went to preschool in knee-pants and the rest of his uniform. An Indian boy who was in his class lived across the street; the two quickly became best friends. They carried on conversations across the road using the telephone they made out of plastic beakers and a long piece of string. Axel Joachim began to put down roots again. When his beloved pet hamster disappeared from its cage he was heartbroken. Leonard helped the boy search the house but the animal had vanished without a trace.

Through friends, Marianne landed a job in a boutique that sold tailored women's clothing. The shop, on Sainte Catherine Street, was run by a fashionista who employed two older seamstresses. In a tailored black dress and hand-sewn white blouse, Marianne was given a dressing down by the boss because she told customers what flattered them and what didn't. She was informed that her job was to sell clothes, not to advise the ladies who came in about what they should wear. But Marianne's customers came back and at the end of the year Marianne was commended for having made more sales than anyone else in the shop.

In the six years that Leonard had spent mostly in Europe, folk music had been enjoying an efflorescence in New York of which he'd scarcely been aware. During a visit to the city, Leonard bumped into people like Bob Dylan and Joan Baez and when he heard them perform it occurred to him that perhaps he too could could be a musician, even though he believed he could barely sing a pure note. He stayed at the Chelsea Hotel, which was frequented by artists like Dylan, Janis Joplin and Andy Warhol.[74] Marianne joined him in New York once in a while, but he usually kept his family life separate from his life as an artist.

After some time in Montreal Leonard made up his mind to seek work as a studio musician in Nashville. On his way south, he stopped in New York, where he met the singer Judy Collins. He played her some of the material he'd been writing. Judy thought the songs were quite good and asked him to keep in touch with her. Leonard ran out of money in New York and never got to Nashville. He headed back to Montreal to scrape together more money.[75]

In Montreal, Marianne grew accustomed to Leonard switching between his typewriter and his guitar as he worked on the many new songs he was writing. On Hydra he'd played for her long before he'd begun to write his own songs and she'd loved to hear him sing and play. Now Leonard's words and melodies were about to reach large audiences.

Spending a long time on everything he created, Leonard didn't think he ever benefitted much from inspiration. Rather, he was inspired by the idea of making something good. The ideas arose from the work itself, and he kept at it until something better than his conception — better than himself — emerged from it. Deep down he believed he was a writer, not a singer or a musician. But writing couldn't sustain his life, and other talents within him sought expression.[76]

While Marianne and Leonard strove to find a common language, the song "Suzanne" came into being. Leonard rang Judy Collins, picked up the guitar and sang it for her over the telephone. She wasted no time in recording it herself.[77]

Leonard was now constantly travelling in connection with his music or his books. The life they'd shared on Hydra — their simple, coordinated daily exertions under the Greek sun — was thousands of miles away. It was as if they were talking past one another: neither of them wholly understood what the other was saying. Living under the same roof became fraught with difficulty.

In the winter of 1966 Marianne wrote to Axel that she and Leonard needed a break from one another and that she was taking Axel Joachim to visit their old friend John in Mexico. Marianne and Axel rarely corresponded anymore and Axel Joachim had no contact with his father. Axel, who was then living, as he himself put it, in the petit bourgeois paradise of Frederikstad, south-east of Oslo, replied that he was impressed to learn of Marianne's globe-trotting. He described his own visit to John and their experimentations. According to Axel, Marianne had much to look forward to:

> One day we ate a mushroom, chewed it pensively
> like a cow and left the rest to chemistry. I discovered
> that I had testicles in my armpits. The word
> Oblomov became Vomolbo and then Voffmobloff
> and ffoblomvoff etc. This kept us going for hours.
> Suddenly I became Buddha . . . Oh, mushrooms! 24
> hours it lasted. I slept and sang arias. Look forward to
> Mexico! And give my regards to John.
> Say hello to Leonard and Little Ax.
> Write and keep in touch. If you could get me a
> sugarcube with LSD25, mescalin or something similar,
> I'd be more than happy, it appears that my latent
> psychosis isn't anything more than gigantic hysterical
> laughter — then silence, from silence to silence,
> forever.
> With regards and blessings!
> Axel
> P.S.
> no P.S.[78]

MEXICO

When Marianne and Axel Joachim arrived, John greeted them from his wheelchair on the veranda of his beautiful villa on a banana plantation. An iguana stuck out its tongue at them and John embraced them warmly. The garden was a little oasis full of banana trees and tropical plants. The bus-ride from Mexico City to Oaxaca had taken several hours and now that they'd arrived Marianne could relax. She was happy to go barefoot again, glad to have left urban life behind and to have come to such an exotic and fascinating place. For Axel Joachim it was like a fairy tale. He bounded around the garden, conversed with the Indian gardener and eventually found a playmate his own age.

John and Marianne enjoyed long conversations while the boy played. Marianne expressed her anxiety about how things would turn out between her and Leonard. John tried to impress on her: "This is here and now. Don't think about anything else. Don't run away again."

Marianne and Axel Joachim slept in dark brown carved four-poster beds. On the night tables lay antivenin pills to be used in case of a scorpion sting. John's housekeeper, who lived in an outbuilding in the garden, cooked and cleaned for him and his guests. The devout woman had once walked on her knees up the mountain to the Holy Virgin Mary, where she'd prayed before returning home with bloody knees.

Under wide-brimmed Mexican hats, the neighbourhood men drank home-distilled tequila. They wore colourful headbands and cropped white pants. The women, whose hair was adorned with beautiful silk ribbons, produced intricate works of art by pressing vividly dyed wool yarn into frames filled with soft wax. Marianne and Axel Joachim visited remote settlements located along narrow roads that wound their way up the mountainside. The houses clung tightly to narrow shelves built on boulders: the rain flowed between the big stones rather than washing away the dwellings. Inside people slept in hammocks. Axel Joachim and

Marianne bought live iguanas from some children they passed on the road and ended up eating the lizards for dinner when the animals refused to eat in captivity. When Leonard rang from New York to hear how they were, Marianne was almost incapable of describing her impressions. Modern civilization seemed like a distant echo.

She thought she'd encountered a culture that had hardly changed in the last century — right up until late one night when she was walking around and she heard a song by Dylan (perhaps at that very moment hanging around with Leonard at the Chelsea Hotel) emanating from a house. At the market they could buy little glow-in-the-dark skeletons and key chains attached to tiny television sets that displayed pictures of nude women. A vast selection of gimcrack souvenirs from the U.S. were arrayed on white cotton sheets on the ground, side by side with horsemeat and home-made cheese. An old woman beckoned Marianne into her primitive shack. The woman pulled a white cotton blouse embroidered with red birds and flowers over Marianne's head and tied a blue striped wrap-around skirt around her waist. Marianne was sent off with her blue jeans and t-shirt rolled up in an old newspaper. She managed to collect her wits and run back to the shop with money. They visited the local church, where the saints were represented by pink plastic dolls that had been painted and dressed up. Jesus was life-sized, complete with glued-on hair and beard, reposing in a glass case.

Marianne dropped acid for the first time, with John in Mexico. Axel was involved in a form of psychotherapy that employed LSD — so-called psycholytic therapy — at the London clinic of the Scottish psychiatrist Ronald David Laing. Laing believed that the treatment quickly opened up the unconscious but that without the benefit of a skilled guide the experience could become a nightmare.[79] Marianne hoped LSD might open her eyes to solutions to the dilemmas she was facing, some way out of the dead-end in which she found herself. John guided her, assuring her that her arms and legs were where they should be when Marianne grew uneasy. Keep cool, he said — tune in, drop out. Marianne felt distressed as control slipped away from her and her emotions were intensified. It was as if all her senses were as tender and exposed as the petals of a water lily floating open on a pond. The material reality that she knew dissolved. Ceilings and walls were no longer where they had been; the floor vanished. Characters from fairy tales and fables appeared, and she wanted to move into the sunset. Some aspects of her trip were so terrifying that she thought she would die, but John reassured her that everything was alright: she could let go, move into the colours and talk to the animals. He was her guide, piloting her through the experience so that she came through it in one piece.

During a subsequent experience with LSD, Marianne watched in the mirror as her face disintegrated. She couldn't put it together again. Looking at her damaged countenance, she told herself that it was just a bad dream. When she came down from the trip she was forced to acknowledge that the simple solutions she'd hoped for did not exist. She never used acid again.

———

During that side trip from Montreal, at a point when her world seemed on the verge of crumbling, Marianne surrendered to the awareness of that something greater than herself. She didn't think she would ever be the same when she came down from those Mexican mountains. She bought herself a beautiful embroidered yellow dress, which she would later wear while Leonard sketched her, sitting on a chair in their house on Hydra. Another purchase was a traditional blanket with the motif of a woman and a man woven in the middle. When she and Axel Joachim came back to Montreal, Leonard and Marianne sat under the blanket in silence. They sat there wordlessly, letting calm settle over them. They had reached a crossroads and the world wasn't going to ruin after all.

TO HYDRA AGAIN

After the trip to Mexico Marianne and Axel Joachim stayed for a short time in Montreal before returning to Hydra. Leonard, who was on tour, wrote in December 1966 from Edmonton that he'd hidden himself away in a little hotel because the crowds were getting too big. During a snowstorm, he'd sought lee from the bitter northerly wind in an entryway. There stood two girls, shivering while they waited for the storm to abate. They had no place to stay. Leonard invited the girls back with him to his modest hotel room. Exhausted from their travels, they immediately fell asleep on his bed. Leonard settled into an old armchair by the radiator. He sat there looking out the window over the frozen North Saskatchewan River and the beautiful northern view. In the double bed the girls slept on. He picked up his guitar and played quietly, so they wouldn't wake up. For the first time in his life, Leonard wrote a song from start to finish without changing a single note afterward. When the girls awoke the next morning, he played "Sisters of Mercy" for them.[80]

In his letter to Marianne, Leonard explains that:

> . . . I was able at last to be what I must be, a singer, a man who owns nothing. I was able to give to over a thousand people the love that I have never been able to place, the ungreedy love which I know can warm the universe. I know now what I must train myself for. I must work, I must be celibate, I must be selfless.
>
> I hope we can repair the painful spaces where uncertainties have led us. I hope you can lead yourself out of despair and I hope I can help you . . .[81]

Leonard is in the process of setting himself free. The letter he writes to Marianne echoes what Axel used to tell her when they were first together: he will lend a hand, but Marianne must help herself. The difference is that Leonard and Marianne no longer have a permanent relationship. She decides that the best she can do for herself and her child is to return to Hydra; perhaps she'll find a future for herself there. Montreal is too lonely without Leonard.

———

To Marianne Cohen
February 23, 1967

Darling,
I sang in New York for the first time last night, at a huge benefit concert. Every singer you've ever heard of was there performing.

Judy Collins introduced me to the audience, over 3000 people, and they seemed to know who I was, mostly because of "Suzanne." I stepped up to the mike, hit a chord on my guitar, found the instrument had gone completely out of tune, tried to tune it, couldn't get more than a croak out of my throat, managed four lines of "Suzanne," my voice unbelievably flat, then I broke off and said simply, "sorry, I just can't make it," and walked off the stage, my fingers like rubber bands, the people baffled and my career in music dying among the coughs of the people backstage. Judy went out and did some more songs while I stood numbly in the wings while a curious happiness seemed to overtake me: I had failed, I had really failed, there is something so beautiful about total failure, it really made me drunk. I found myself walking on stage again and I managed to squeeze "Stranger song" out of my throat. I hardly got the words out, the throat and the guitar broke down completely several times, but I finished somehow and I thought I'll just commit suicide. Nobody really knew what to do or say. I think that someone took my hand and led me off, the triumphant in my shame, and I think I heard some people shout Bravo or maybe they were just clearing their throats. Everybody back stage very sorry for me and they couldn't believe how happy I was, how relieved I was that it had all come to nothing, that I had never been so free. However the 13 year olds apparently liked it — I'm doing an interview with the Hit Parader, and for all I know a cult may grow around this disaster.

This damn hotel, loneliness, isolation, insomnia, the secular triumph that always just misses me — it's all made me calm and curiously happy, it's all mine at last, it's my kingdom.

I should be there in a month or so to see what I can do with another book. I hope you're feeling good, little friend of my life, I love it when you're happy. Axel's card was beautiful, hug him from me.

Goodnight darling,

Leonard[82]

MILITARY JUNTA

In April 1967 a cabal of colonels seized control of Greece, overthrowing the government and establishing rule by the military junta. Leonard was in America, where he'd been for some time, when the coup d'état took place, while Marianne was staying at a hotel in Athens, along with friends from Hydra. Following several days of unrest, news of the regime change was announced over the Greek radio. The band of Hydra friends was informed at the hotel's reception desk. Hearing shots outside, they ran up the fire stairs to the roof to see what was going on. From their vantage point at the top of the hotel in Syntagma Square, in the heart of the city, they looked down on streets empty of people but swarming with tanks. More shots were fired. Marianne was struck by the perilousness of the situation and wondered what would happen next.

They holed up in the hotel for three days before venturing out to Piraeus to board the ferry home. When they got off the boat at Hydra, they were instructed to register at the police station. There were three times as many policemen as usual on the island. Rather than lazing in the spring sunshine over a glass of retsina or a Greek coffee at the port, people did their errands and darted silently home again through the oppressive atmosphere.

Under the dictatorship, all foreigners were required to have a residence permit and had to prove that they weren't employed in Greece and that the money they lived on came from abroad. Marianne obtained a red slip of paper from the bank stating that the funds in her account came from outside the country and delivered it to the police. Hunting rifles and knives — anything that resembled a weapon — had to be relinquished to the authorities. Marianne handed in an old bayonet and its sheath that belonged to Leonard. When she was called on the carpet at the police station, she had with her Axel Joachim and some other children she was looking after. It was a drawn-out affair and the children cavorted and couldn't sit still. To bring it to an end, Marianne pulled "a Greek one," wailing for all she was worth while the tears streamed down her face — exactly as she had done when she'd studied the role of Hedvig in *The Wild Duck*. The men couldn't bear female hysterics and asked her to take the children and leave.

The persistent flow of threats issued by the police and the general air of menace subdued and constrained the social life of the foreigners on Hydra. They had once been on relaxed, friendly terms with the police, often sharing a carafe of retsina at a taverna with them. Now the expatriates were stopped on their way to or from the port and constantly found notices on their doors directing them to report to the station at such and such a time.

New arrivals had to register with the police and officers in plain-clothes strolled the streets and sat at café tables to spy on them. One day while Marianne was at the port a young man who had just come from Athens sat at one of the other café tables. He was loud and jovial and took no notice of Marianne's attempts to signal that he was being observed by a policeman. By the time the young man got back to his hotel the police had searched his room. Without the benefit of a lawyer, he was convicted of possessing narcotics. He was sent to prison on the island of Aegina, the first stop on the ferry from Athens to Hydra. The place was notorious for its short rations and bad treatment of prisoners.

Strict censoring was introduced in the country. Many Left-leaning politicians and union people were arrested; thousands of Greeks were tortured. In league with his prime minister, the king attempted to muster a counter-coup later that year but it was a fiasco and he was forced to flee to Italy with his family.

Far from troubled Greece, Leonard was often touring as his singing and songwriting career took wing. He and Marianne kept in touch by letter and telegram. In April 1967, the same month that the military junta seized power in Greece, Leonard wrote several letters to Marianne at brief intervals:

April 9

Darling,
    We need to be with each other this minute,
nothing to say, but I want to be talking to you now,
so this letter, another part of our mysterious enduring
love.
    I put steel strings on my guitar, that's like changing
from underwear to armour, that's New York City.
Given up plans for sainthood, revolution, redemptive
visions, music mastery, just the ageing man with a
notebook, happiest when alone in a Puerto Rican

restaurant, coffee and Spanish juke-box, and I've crossed the equator of my very cold heart and I'm a human again, a second here and there.

. . . Someone in Hollywood wants to buy Suzanne. Buffy Ste Marie doing Stranger and a new song. Nico, Andy Warhol's star, recording a new song called The Jewels in Your Shoulder. Offers from Expo, Newport Folk Festival, a tour in the Fall of forty American colleges, this last thing involves too much to even think about. Very anxious to write a book before it starts.

Tell me about Axel. Give him my blessings and love. I can't help thinking that a New York slum is the best place for him, or if not that, a farm.

Such beautiful music on the radio. I want to put away my guitar and just listen to the way they sing and the way they talk. Talked to an old man last night in the cafeteria, 67 years old, merchant seaman, told me he had 500 dollars in his pocket. He said, "Many a true word has passed through these false teeth."

Walking through the city, insisting that no one follow, feeling either black or golden, dead to lust, tired of ambition, a lazy student of my own pain, happy about the occasional sun, thin and dressing very shabbily, hair out of control, feeling good tonight as I write my perfect friend.

The radio says it's almost morning, the hotel window doesn't connect with the sky so I'm never sure. How is Sophia? I'd love to hear that you and Axel and Sophia are strong and happy.

Isn't it curious and warm to grow old in each other's life?

All my love,

Leonard[83]

April 12, 1967

Seven o' clock in the morning, the news says it's 29
degrees, cold when I crossed the street for a morning
strawberry milkshake, thinking about changing the
steel strings back to the old softer ones, smoking
Turkish cigarettes, the crysanthemums I bought myself
some weeks ago, mauve, rust and yellow, are dry and
fragile, and something in me rests every time I look
at them, it's good to be at my desk so early in the day
with you and words on my mind, I put on a shirt and
tie this morning and a string of Indian bells around my
neck, I don't think I ever wrote a tune, I just found
some tunes that were already there, I keep a candle
burning all the time in my room, a tall green candle in
a glass, dedicated to St. Jude Thaddeus, Patron Saint
of Impossible Causes . . . well, good morning darling,
something about the thought of you is so sweet, even
our old battle cries seem like bells.[84]

SUMMERHILL

Axel Joachim sprang barefoot from house to house along with his
playmates, who came from countries all over the world. A young
German visiting the island took the boy up to the cloister on the
mountain and taught him to play the flute. Axel Joachim had stars
in his eyes when he came back in the afternoon. He said that he
now carried not only Jesus in his heart but Buddha as well. Later,
when he wanted to know how babies came into being, Marianne
began by putting a sheet of paper on the kitchen table and drawing
a little boy and girl, explaining that they were inside the womb of
their mother. Axel Joachim listened carefully before he took the
pen out of her hand and leaned across the table. Drawing a line
from the heads of the two figures, he extended the line across the

table and as far as he could reach up the whitewashed wall. When his mother asked what he'd drawn, Axel Joachim explained that it was the children's antennae to God.

At seven, Axel Joachim was now of school age. While the three children of George and Charmian went to the local school, along with the Greek children, the daughters of Marianne and Leonard's friend Demetri Gassoumis went to Summerhill, a boarding school in Suffolk, England. Many of the school's teachers had visited Hydra and had social connections there. Summerhill was a phenomenon in the 1960s and its controversial educational principles were even being talked about in Norway. The institution's founder, Alexander Sutherland Neill, was of the radical opinion that the school should adapt to the pupil, rather than the other way around. Like many others, Marianne believed that Summerhill was a good alternative to conventional schooling or the kind of education her son would get on Hydra. Physically his father's spirit and image, the boy had always had a good head on his shoulders and was a quick learner. He spoke three languages fluently and was experienced in meeting people from all over the world. Marianne was convinced that Summerhill was the right choice for her son and by the time Leonard came back to Hydra in the summer of 1967, they'd been notified that Axel Joachim had been admitted.

One morning they looked out the window at the new telephone lines strung in front of their house. Leonard had settled on Hydra with the notion that he'd traded the modern world for a simpler, more authentic kind of life. He used to look out at the blooming almond tree while he wrote. Now the cables that criss-crossed the view were like a symbol that modernity had, inexorably, reached them. Birds alighted like musical notes on the new lines. Marianne made a cup of cacao for Leonard, who'd been ill, and lifted the guitar down from the wall for him. He strummed it and said, "Like a bird on the wire."

Leonard took Axel Joachim to England for his first day of school at the end of the summer. "I'm coming back soon,

Mummy," promised the little boy as he departed in his blue jeans and denim jacket. Marianne swallowed the lump in her throat as she watched her son padding off hand in hand with Leonard.

Leonard, who had travelled onward from England to New York, reassured Marianne that all was well with her son. The boy had shed a few tears on the plane from Athens, but when Leonard had parted with Axel Joachim at the school, he was sitting happily in a treehouse in the company of Athene, Demetri's eldest daughter, who was about his age, and a couple of other children. Marianne was not to worry: Leonard believed Axel would be fine at Summerhill. He had paid for the first semester and the school would buy pyjamas and anything else Axel Joachim lacked and would add the expenses to their account.

But Axel wasn't happy at Summerhill. Written in his crooked, childish hand, his letters to his mother told her that that he missed her, he didn't have many friends, the bigger boys were rough on him. He asked her to send presents that he could dole out to his schoolmates so they wouldn't bother him. Axel Joachim also wrote to Leonard, who was staying on Bleecker Street in New York:

> Dear Leonard,
> I miss you. On the way back from New York to Greece come and see me if you can stay in England. Come and pick me up. I hope to go back in the same plane with you. It's warm and nice here. Sometimes it is cold. Can I travel with a little wooden suitcase which I am making in woodwork? It has got a lock on it. And I want an answer to this letter.
> Love and kisses xxxxx Axel[85]

Marianne's heart sank when she read Axel Joachim's letters, but she hoped that with time he would find his feet. She made trips to London so she could see him during day and weekend visits. The first time she visited Summerhill, she had an appointment with the headmaster and founder. She sat on a swing in the garden and swung back and forth while she waited until it was time for the meeting. When she entered the office in the venerable old brick building, Neill wondered if it had been her swinging under the tree outside.

"Yes," Marianne replied.

"I thought it was one of the pupils," he rejoined, making Marianne feel like a child.

During these visits Axel Joachim didn't say much about how he was faring, and Marianne didn't realize how strongly the boy wanted to leave the school. There were many gifted children at Summerhill and she was convinced it was the best option for her son. She would later suffer a deep sense of guilt for having sent him away instead of protecting him and providing him with a more stable upbringing.

FAREWELL TO GEORGE AND CHARMIAN

There had been many changes in the social scene on Hydra since Marianne had first arrived in December 1957. Marianne was one of the few who remained of the core of foreign permanent residents on the island. The people who passed through Hydra were on manifold life journeys and the friends were used to letting each other go.

George Johnston was now gravely ill. Fourteen years after he and Charmian left Australia, the couple decided to return to their homeland. The Johnstons had been pioneers among the foreigners and Marianne had watched their three children grow up. She had also witnessed their ruination over the years.

In 1969, two years after the Johnstons left Hydra for good, Charmian killed herself. It was the eve of the publication of her husband's novel, *Clean Straw for Nothing*. The book partly concerned the infidelities of the protagonist's wife, a character recognizable as Charmian. In his biography, *Charmian and*

George, Max Brown quotes the note Charmian left behind for her husband: "Darling, Sorry about this. I can't stand being hated — and you hated me so much today — I am opting out and you can play it any way you wish from now on. I am sure you will have a most successful and distinguished career."[86] One year later George succumbed to tuberculosis.

In the autumn of 1967 Leonard was in a studio in New York recording his first album, *Songs of Leonard Cohen*, which would be in the stores in December. Leonard wrote to Marianne that it was going well in the studio and they often worked through the night and into the morning hours. But he didn't know what he should write to her anymore — everything was too little or too much.[87]

An unpublished poem he composed that year expresses much of what he felt for Marianne:

The Poetry Place

This is for you
it is my full heart
it is the book I meant to read you
when we were old
Now I am a shadow
I am restless as an empire
You are the woman
who released me
I saw you watching the moon
you did not hesitate
to love me with it
I saw you honouring the wind-flowers
caught in the rocks
you loved me with them
At night I saw you dance alone
on the small wet pebbles
of the shoreline

and you welcomed me into the circle
more than a guest
All this happened
in the truth of time
in the truth of flesh
I saw you with a child
you brought me to his perfume
and his visions
without demand of blood
On so many wooden tables
adorned with food and candles
a thousand sacraments
which you carried in your basket
I visited my clay
I visited my birth
and you guarded my back
as I became small
and frightened enough
to be born again
I wanted you for your beauty
and you gave me more than yourself
you shared your beauty
this I only learned tonight
as I recall the mirrors
you walked away from
after you had given them
whatever they claimed
for my initiation
Now I am a shadow
I long for the boundaries
of my wandering
and I move
with the energy of your prayer
for you are kneeling

like a bouquet
in a cave of a bone
behind my forehead
and I move toward a love
you have dreamed for me[88]

Marianne read this by chance many years later.

AUSTIN DELANEY

Marianne had never fully reconciled herself to Axel's abandonment while she was at her most vulnerable, caring for a newborn
baby. Nonetheless, she bore within her the positive aspects of
Axel. She had learned something about how great, and how petty,
life could be. She had let love determine the course of her life
and had gained an understanding of love that she carried into her
relationship with Leonard. John Starr Cooke had once written to
her that "to fall in love" was an awful expression in the English
language. He thought that it should be to "rest" in love or to "lean
onto" love. John believed that people have a fundamental fear of
falling and being without support, and he couldn't comprehend
why people were dead set on *falling* in love.

Slowly, weightlessly, the relationship between Marianne and
Leonard collapsed, like ashes falling to the ground. There were
no confrontations, few discussions. The periods of separation
grew longer and longer, the distance between them lengthened.
Both were striving to find their ways of living, Marianne with her
child, Leonard with his writing and music.

As her relationship with Leonard languished, she felt the urge
to confide in Axel. Axel lived an unconventional life himself,
and she knew he would be open to her thoughts. Maybe he could
offer her advice, as he had continually done when they'd been
together. Axel had left Lena and the children in Fredriskstad and
moved into a fisherman's shack on the coast of Helgeland, on the

western coast of Norway, to write. Marianne and Axel, licking
their wounds, exchanged letters from the northern and southern
ends of Europe.

> It's painful to read that you and Leonard aren't making
> it together, and I don't know what to say, I don't know
> your relationship, know only that I have sprung a leak
> with Lena, and the ship is listing badly, maybe it will
> sink, and the captain is standing on the bridge and
> saluting. Around me the night is blue, everything is
> still, a bird screeches now and then, or is it a song? I
> am alone here and am working on Lem, the second
> volume of Epp, as I'm sure I've told you. I think it's
> going fairly well, well, we'll see. Now the birds are
> singing, yes, it must be a song, so much of the night
> has passed that it's sliding toward day now. I live in
> a little shack, two rooms, cook for myself, when the
> water boils in the pot, my brain is often also boiling . . .
> Yesterday I plucked bluebells and daisies. The
> bluebells are standing in water on the writing table,
> they tremble when I type on the machine. What
> else? Small fishing vessels in the harbour, islets and
> skerries, cloudberries in the bog, tarns, woods, I could
> buy a cheap farm here, many acres of land, a little
> harbour with boat sheds, big house, barn, I could be
> a seaside farmer and be self-sufficient here for ten or
> fifteen thousand kroner, I'm thinking of it. Farmer and
> fisherman in the summertime and bookman during
> the dark winter, why not? . . .
> Dear Marianne, live well. Say hello to Little Axel,
> and give Leonard my regards. I don't know what you
> should do. Send me a few lines when you feel like it,
> it would make me happy. The address is: Axel Jensen,
> Kirkøy, Vega, Norway.

Think of me when you bathe in Hydrawater.
Axel[89]

Axel couldn't provide Marianne with any answers. On Hydra she delved into Jung's dream interpretations, which Axel had introduced her to as long ago as 1955. Jung had employed the Chinese divination book *I Ching (Book of Changes)* as a tool for self-discovery, and Leonard and Axel — both of whom had been preoccupied with the volume long before they came to Greece — used to discuss it when Marianne was still married to Axel. Marianne's worn copy, which had a foreword by Jung, was heavily marked up with handwritten annotations. Rooted in ancient Chinese philosophy, the three-thousand-year-old work presents the meanings of sixty-four hexagrams, each of which stands for a life situation. To determine their hexagrams, Marianne, Axel and Leonard tossed three special coins into the air and let them land on the table. The two sides of the coins had different values, and when they had been cast six times the six lines of the hexagram were drawn. It was then a matter of deciphering the book's explanation for that figure and extracting the answers they were looking for. The expatriates on Hydra dipped into diverse esoteric pursuits, sometimes using them to find solutions when they wound up in thorny situations, often because of infidelity.

One day a man by the name of Austin Delaney arrived on Hydra bearing a suitcase full of toys. Delaney had saved his earnings as a doorman and bartender so he could train as a psychoanalyst at the Jung Institute in Switzerland. Before coming to Greece he had practised in India, where he'd observed how children reveal their internal troubles through their play. Marianne had recently had an intense dream in which she stood in a field, newly ploughed with deep furrows. She wore a faded orange shirt that belonged to Leonard. Looking down, she saw her penis falling to the ground and awoke with a start. The field had been one she had known in Larkollen; she'd earned pocket money there during the summer, picking cucumbers. Unable to get the dream out of her thoughts, she told Delaney that she wanted to go into therapy with him. He took her on immediately.

Delaney had made a sandbox in the house he rented; around the frame of the box lay dolls, tin soldiers, matchboxes, candlesticks and a variety of other playthings and objects from his suitcase. He instructed Marianne that she could do whatever she liked in the sandbox. Marianne was at a loss. In the end she made a little altar in the sand, where she buried her ring and lit a candle. Austin said nothing and Marianne went home.

When she came back for the next session, she admitted that she hadn't been honest: what she'd really wanted to do was to pee in Delaney's sandbox.

"Now we can get down to work," said Delaney. "When are you going to do what you *really* want?"

Marianne filled several notebooks with descriptions of her dreams and met regularly with her psychoanalyst. She felt she was approaching a turning point in her self-understanding. After five weeks in therapy with Delaney she wrote to Leonard, telling him that she'd never before managed to shed as much light on her dreams as now. Delaney was returning to Zurich, she explained, but Marianne felt she couldn't stop the work. She hoped to spend a couple of months — or however long it took — in Switzerland, continuing her therapy. Axel Joachim wished very much to be together with Leonard for a month or two during his summer holiday. It would be a great help to her and the boy if this could be arranged, Marianne said. She could take him with her to Zurich, but Axel Joachim strongly needed a father figure in his life now. Delaney had promised to help find her paid work in Zurich, and she planned to take her car so she could stay in cheaper accommodations outside the city. She'd also been thinking of going to India, but she didn't think she had enough money for that and, besides, the inner work had to be done here. Marianne told Leonard that she was convinced that she was on her way to becoming a whole person.

Chapter 13

NEW YORK

Austin Delaney took his suitcase and went back to Zurich, leaving the empty sandbox behind on Hydra. Leonard hadn't been able to take Axel Joachim for the long period Marianne had proposed so she dropped her plans to follow Delaney to Switzerland to continue her therapy there.

To get away from Hydra, Marianne went to New York, where Demetri Gassoumis and his daughters — Axel Joachim's schoolmates at Summerhill — were now living. Marianne's friend from Montreal, Carol Zemel, was also moving to the city. Leonard was based there too. Paying low rent for a loft available through friends of friends, Marianne, Axel Joachim and Carol moved onto Clinton Street on the Lower East Side, one of the poorest parts of town. The loft apartment, which they'd taken over from a painter, had a kitchen and bathroom in one end and two bedrooms at the other end. In between lay a large, long room. Windows along the length of the apartment looked down over a big schoolyard.

Carol was studying art history at Columbia University while Marianne stayed at home. Demetri and his family moved into another loft three blocks up the street, above The Puerto Rican Magic Store, where Marianne bought candles in glass containers adorned with images of the patron saint of hopeless causes. She and Carol were always burning candles, on the table or in one of the many windowsills facing the school.

New York was a big city and everything was new to Marianne. The district of Manhattan in which they found themselves had once been the Jewish quarter of the city. Now it was Puerto Rican. The synagogues were closed and the neighbourhood was rife with poverty and alcohol abuse. People set fire to their apartments as a strategem to get better housing. Artists and musicians were moving into the old lofts that had once been tailors' workshops and sweatshops of various kinds.

At night, while Carol stayed home with Axel Joachim, Marianne and her French friend Jean Marc Appert earned money on 42nd Street by selling small cats they fashioned on the spot. Jean Marc was an old friend from Hydra who was staying with Marianne and Carol. He had come to New York from South America, where he'd paddled a canoe along great lengths of the Amazon River. The police gave them permission to peddle their goods on the sidewalk after the shops had closed for the evening. Feeling marvellously free, Marianne wondered what her parents would think if they could see her. The cats were modelled from steel wire and wool yarn and had whiskers and small felt eyes. Some had long tails — ideal for back-scratching, as Marianne told the curious nightclub, restaurant and bar patrons who passed by. Sales were good. This wasn't the best part of town, and being a street vendor was a world away from the rustic domestic life Marianne had enjoyed on Hydra. Leonard felt she was too pure for this debauched existence in New York and wished he could shield her from it.

Axel Joachim was nine years old and was enrolled in school along with Demetris' two girls. Children of diverse nationalities attended the school, which had a rough climate. Going to the bathroom was not permitted without an escort and the older pupils inveigled the younger ones into taking pills and smoking hash. But Axel Joachim's teacher, Mrs. Hawkins, cared for her charges and the boy was an apt pupil and soon settled in. The three Hydra children stuck together. They did their homework together and slept at one another's homes. Axel Joachim's best friend from Hydra lived just outside the city and the two of them often spent the weekend together. In his aeronautical phase, Axel Joachim decorated the walls of his room with his illustrations of the interior of a space ship. Surrounded by drawings of instruments and buttons, it was just a matter of sitting in the cockpit and zooming off into outer space.

Being surrounded by impoverishment had its effect on them. Axel Joachim frequently came home with a new friend with whom he wanted to share his food and toys because the child had been beaten by his alcoholic father or his family was in disarray.

Marianne visited Leonard's sister Esther, who lived in one of the better neighbourhoods Uptown. Mostly Marianne socialized with Hydra friends. Central Park was their playground, where they gathered every Sunday with the children. Norman Peterson, a sculptor Marianne knew from the island, lived under the Brooklyn Bridge. On Hydra he'd collected empty tin cans and transformed them into art. There he'd lived in a windowless, doorless concrete shell known as the crash pad. On cold days he dragged a tree trunk inside, which he burned bit by bit. Before he came to Hydra he'd built a house out of driftwood on the coast of California; the sale of the house had given him the funds to travel to Hydra. In New York Norman again gathered driftwood, out of which he made exquisite furniture.

Some days Marianne took the children to the cinema, where they often watched several films in a row. People used the movie house as a place to sleep and eat — it was a roof over their heads, for a few hours. One late night when she and Jean Marc came home from the Andy Warhol film *Sleep* — five hours of footage of a man sleeping — they were accosted by two men at the door to the apartment building. Jean Marc put up resistance until a large knife appeared from the layers of a folded newspaper. Marianne was scared stiff and gave them all the money she had in her wallet. Faint with fear, she heard her own voice saying mechanically,

"Why did you have to frighten the shit out of me — why didn't you just ask for the money?" There was silence for a few seconds and then one of the men said to the other, "This chick is cool. Let's split!" The door banged shut behind them.

It took a long time for Marianne to get over her fear of being robbed in her own doorway. She became afraid to go out in the streets alone and always asked cab drivers to wait until the door had closed behind her. She had once wandered the streets of New York with her head in the clouds, daydreaming. It was time to plant her feet solidly back on the ground and her head on her shoulders.

Marianne embarked on a body-oriented form of psychotherapy with the celebrated psychotherapist Alexander Lowen. A student of the Freudian Wilhelm Reich, Lowen had developed his mind–body method in the 1960s. Marianne had tried a variety of alternative therapies, including the sandbox on Hydra and Jungian dream interpretation. Now she learned that "the body remembers everything," as they worked with a mix of breathing and movement exercises, along with conversational therapy.

———

Janis Joplin used to drop coins in a jukebox in a little bar near the apartment block where Marianne lived, and Bob Dylan bought shoes in a shop that belonged to a friend of hers. One day Marianne's bus stopped farther than usual from the curb. As she descended from the lowest step of the bus, expecting to set her foot on the sidewalk, she pitched forward. The first thing she saw was a pair of pointy black shoes, then white trousers and a white jacket. Recovering her balance, she found herself looking right into Bob Dylan's face. He smiled, still holding her arm to support her. "Thank you," she said, and then blurted, "Oh, you look like Bob Dylan." "It's me, ma'am," he replied. Marianne bowed politely and went on her way down the street. The store she headed to was run by a friend of the Beat poet Allen Ginsberg.

It sold everything from handcarved walking sticks to first editions and container finds. "Too bad you didn't come a little earlier," said her friend the shopkeeper, "then you would have gotten to meet Bob Dylan."

When the Hare Krishna movement arrived in New York, Marianne and her friends joined a crowd in Tompkins Square Park, where the spiritual leader Prabhupada and his disciples sat under a big elm tree and had their first "chanting session" outside India. It was October 9th, 1966 — the start of the Hare Krishna religious movement in the U.S. The crowd chanted for two hours. They danced and played cymbals, tambourines and other instruments. Marianne sang rhythmically: *Hare Krishna, Hare Krishna, Krishna Krishna, Hare Hare, Hare Rama, Hare Rama, Rama Rama, Hare Hare . . .* The shared mantra and feeling of collectivity made a powerful impression on Marianne.

Leonard took Marianne to a Janis Joplin concert in Madison Square Garden. The audience was wild and a young man in the first row managed to throw himself onto the stage and cling to the singer's hair. Joplin swung him back and forth a few times before security guards came to her rescue. Marianne also went with Leonard to the Chelsea Hotel several times and met luminaries like Andy Warhol, Buffy Sainte-Marie and Joni Mitchell. But Marianne's contact with Leonard was limited. He visited them on Clinton Street, but refrained from drawing Marianne and Axel Joachim into his life. "This isn't your scene, Marianne," he advised her.

Marianne understood why he hadn't taken them with him to New York when he first moved here. The Bohemian lifestyle — the dope and parties — was incompatible with an orderly family life. There were women who followed him wherever he went. Even before Marianne and Carol knew the number of the newly installed telephone in their own apartment, women were calling to get in touch with Leonard. Marianne didn't know Leonard's women or have any connection to the life he led when he wasn't with her. Yet Leonard continued to provide for Marianne and Axel Joachim, paying their rent and the boy's school expenses. For many years after they finally parted ways as lovers, Leonard would take care of Marianne and her son, putting himself at their disposal when they needed help.

Marianne and Axel Joachim spent a little over a year in New York before returning to Europe.

TIME TO TURN BACK

After their stay in New York, Marianne and Axel Joachim divided their time between Larkollen and Hydra. Marianne found it difficult to settle down permanently in Norway after all the years she'd spent abroad. Norway felt almost foreign to her; she longed for the people and the familiar rhythm of life she'd known in Greece. As Leonard used to say, "When you've lived on Hydra, you can't live anywhere else, including Hydra."

In 1972 she and twelve-year-old Axel Joachim were back on the Greek island for the last time as residents. The boy was being tutored privately and they lived in the old house they'd shared with Leonard, who was there very rarely.

One day there was a knock at the door. Marianne opened the door to a young woman with an infant in her arms. The woman wanted to know when Marianne and her son were moving out, so she and her child could move in. It was Suzanne and the baby was her and Leonard's son Adam. Looking at the younger woman, Marianne felt older and stronger, untroubled and strangely relieved. It was time to free herself and get started on her own life's journey.

A little voice inside her said, "Turn back now. Put on your sandals and go home."

Days of Kindness

Greece is a good place
to look at the moon, isn't it
You can read by moonlight
You can read on the terrace
You can see a face
as you saw it when you were young
There was good light then
oil lamps and candles
and those little flames
that floated on a cork in olive oil
What I loved in my old life
I haven't forgotten
It lives in my spine
Marianne and the child
The days of kindness
It rises in my spine
and it manifests as tears
I pray that loving memory
exists for them too
the precious ones I overthrew
for an education in the world

Hydra, 1985[90]

AUTHOR'S EPILOGUE

Marianne has spread out her past on the dining table. She hunts for her glasses and dives into an old cardboard box. It smells of cellar and yellowed, faded sheets of paper. Leafing through piles of photographs and thin light-blue airmail envelopes — letters from family, friends and old lovers — she reads and mumbles half-aloud. Remembering and piecing together far-off times.

"It hasn't been that easy putting myself back in the fifties and sixties. A lot of water has gone under the bridge in half a century. Some things I swept under the carpet back then because they were too difficult to face, and other things I've just plain forgotten until now. For many years I swallowed everything that happened in my life without self-awareness."

The years spent in Greece are distant. More than fifty years have passed since Marianne met Axel and Leonard. When Marianne moved back to Norway for good at the beginning of the 1970s she quickly found work and Axel Joachim began school. The Norwegian Oil Fairy Tale had begun and Marianne landed a job with Norwegian Contractors, a company that built off-shore oil platforms. She worked in the personnel and foreign departments. The bulk of her working career has been in the oil branch, a great contrast to her life on Hydra, where Marianne filled roles as muse, mother and housewife and lived out the love that her writer friends wrote about.

Marianne met her husband Jan Kielland Stang while she was employed at Norwegian Contractors. He was an engineer in the same company and had three daughters from an earlier marriage. They married in 1979 and have been together ever since.

As she approached retirement, Marianne worked with actress Juni Dahr, who toured with her solo shows *Ibsen's Women* and *Joan of Arc* in the U.S., Japan and Europe. Marianne was responsible for making travel arrangements and liasing with the embassies.

"It would take many years before I got hold of my own creativity and began to make pictures. Many with titles from Leonard's songs. I find a lot of unusual things washed up on the shore at Larkollen and I've mounted these in glass cases with small, beautiful gifts I've received through the years."

Now she spends much of her time at her house in Larkollen, where she lived as a little girl with her grandmother.

With a quick motion she opens the door to the little garden and walks toward the sea. Stops before a little green tussock and bends forward. In a moment she shouts:

"Know what I found? Two four-leafed clovers! Hey — here's another one!"

"That means luck, doesn't it?"

"It does. It's rare to find them and it's loaded with them here! Maybe it's just that I see more clearly in my old age?"

MARIANNE'S EPILOGUE

My wonderful grandmother once said: "You will meet a man who speaks with a golden tongue." As always, she was right. I met, in fact, two such men.

If the transition to life in Norway was difficult for me, it was even more problematic for my son. Axel Joachim was swept along on my turbulent journey, but as a child with a sensitive, impressionable mind, he lacked the tools to cope with his experiences in the same way that I could. The difficulties that have persisted into his adulthood have compelled me to question myself continually, and to ask whether the price he paid for my insecurity and vulnerability was too dear. Jan, my husband during the last thirty-four years, developed a close relationship to Axel Joachim and has been an inestimable support for him. For this I am deeply grateful to Jan.

A seed was planted on Hydra. Something germinated, and emerging from grief and loss, at last, I found my way back — home. At the Centre for Growth in Denmark, established by Jes Bertelsen and Hanne Kizach, meditation became the tool that brought me to my inner self, as my grandmother had tried to teach me as we sat feeding the birds at the threshold of the big house in Larkollen during the war. While Leonard went the Zen Way, I took the Tibetan Way.

We never let go of Hydra, our "second home," nor all the people who had meant so much to us. At first we communicated by "snail mail." Later there were meetings in Oslo and Hydra, a place to which I must return every year. So many of us have gone and a new generation has taken over the island. Things change but remain the same.

When I first met the highly accomplished radio journalist Kari Hesthamar in May 2005 the time had finally come for me to delve deeply into the past — that part of my life when I was young, naive, beautiful and vulnerable, with little grasp of myself. Some acts of my Greek drama were so painful that I wished I could forget them. Yet my mature voice came through in the radio documentary that was aired by the Norwegian Broadcasting Corporation in September that same year. The responses I received from friends and strangers showed me that I was not alone: others recognized themselves in my story.

Marianne Ihlen
Oslo, 28 November 2011

ACKNOWLEDGEMENTS

Thank you, Marianne, for so generously sharing your story and your time. This book could not have existed without your indefatigable help.

Thank you, Leonard, for answering my questions with such patience and for letting me use your previously unpublished letters, telegrams, poems and doodles.

Thank you, Prathiba Jensen, for allowing me to reproduce Axel's old letters. It has been like diving into a treasure chest.

A big thanks to the publisher of the Norwegian edition of this book, Frode Molven, for asking me if I would write this after hearing the radio documentary about Marianne and Leonard that was aired by the Norwegian Broadcasting Corporation.

I thank the Norwegian Non-fiction Writers and Translators Association for a writing grant.

Thanks to everyone else who has, in some way, contributed to this book.

And to Knut — my warm gratitude for all your support.

Kari Hesthamar
Oslo, 18 August 2008

TRANSLATOR'S NOTE

When Marianne rang me a few years ago I had neither seen nor spoken to her since I'd been a small girl living on Hydra with my Danish mother, my American father and my little sister. I had come to the island as an infant in 1966; when we left for the U.S. in 1972 I'd finished first grade under the stern-but-kind supervision of Kyria Eleni, who taught at the one-room schoolhouse where I was the only foreigner. I returned to Hydra many times yet I never crossed paths with Marianne. And suddenly there she was, in Oslo, calling me at my adopted home in northern Norway, on an island hundreds of kilometres north of the Arctic Circle, asking if I remembered her.

I'm so grateful that Marianne tracked me down. Working on Kari Hesthamar's book has transported me back to my childhood and to the youth of my parents, when in my eyes they sparkled with the gold dust that Leonard Cohen so eloquently observed to be the property of the young, beautiful, talented people who settled on Hydra in that period.

For their help, I thank my husband, Jon Winther-Hansen; my sister, Johanne Rosenthal; my mother-in-law, Marit Winther Hansen; and my friends Ivar Stokkeland, Alison Leslie Gold, Michaela Hermann and Vicky Ioannidou.

My greatest debt is to my mother, Ane Marie Torp Albertsen. Rie (as she was known) placed her knowledge of Hydra and the Norwegian language (in particular, the "New Norwegian" version of the language, in which Kari wrote *So Long, Marianne*) at my disposal. She collaborated tirelessly and enthusiastically with me until the morning her life was cut unexpectedly short. I have completed the work by carrying Rie constantly in my heart and mind.

Helle Valborg Goldman
Tromsø, 9 June 2013

ENDNOTES

CHAPTER 1

1. Page 14, *A Girl I Knew*. Axel Jensen. New York: Alfred A. Knopf, 1962.
2. *Livet Sett fra Nimbus*. Petter Mejlænder. Oslo: Spartacus, 2002.
3. Niels Christian Brøgger, "Litterært eksperiment," *Nationen*, 21 December 1955.
4. Private letters of Marianne Ihlen.
5. Private letters of Marianne Ihlen.
6. Private letters of Marianne Ihlen.
7. Private letters of Marianne Ihlen.
8. *Livet Sett fra Nimbus*.
9. Private letters of Marianne Ihlen.
10. Private letters of Marianne Ihlen, used with permission of Prathiba Jensen.
11. Private letters of Marianne Ihlen.
12. Private letters of Marianne Ihlen.

CHAPTER 2

13. Private letters of Marianne Ihlen, used with permission of Prathiba Jensen.
14. Delphi, accessed on the internet at www.abrock.com/Greece-Turkey/Olym .html.

CHAPTER 3

15. Funerary customs — *Bli Kjent med Hellas*. Ingunn Kvisterøy and Johan Henrik Schreiner. Oslo: Forlaget Hera, 1987.
16. Page 55, *The Colossus of Maroussi*. Henry Miller. San Francisco: Colt Press, 1941.
17. Private letters of Marianne Ihlen, used with permission of Prathiba Jensen.
18. Private letters of Else Berit and Per Schioldborg.
19. Private letters of Marianne Ihlen, used with permission of Prathiba Jensen.

CHAPTER 4

20. Private letters of Else Berit and Per Schioldborg.
21. Private letters of Marianne Ihlen, used with permission of Prathiba Jensen.
22. Private letters of Marianne Ihlen.
23. Private letters of Marianne Ihlen, used with permission of Prathiba Jensen.
24. Author's interview with Leonard Cohen, Los Angeles, October 2005.
25. Author's interview with Leonard Cohen, Los Angeles, October 2005.
26. Author's interview with Leonard Cohen, Los Angeles, October 2005, and *Various Positions: A Life of Leonard Cohen*. Ira B. Nadel. New York: Pantheon Books, 1996.
27. Author's interview with Leonard Cohen, Los Angeles, October 2005.

CHAPTER 5

28. Author's interview with Leonard Cohen, Los Angeles, October 2005.
29. Private letters of Marianne Ihlen.
30. Private letters of Marianne Ihlen.
31. Private letters of Marianne Ihlen.
32. Private letters of Leonard Cohen.
33. Private letters of Marianne Ihlen.
34. "Dress Rehearsal Rag," on *Songs of Love and Hate*, released by Columbia Records in 1971.

CHAPER 6

35. *Various Positions.*

36. Author's interview with Leonard Cohen, Los Angeles, October 2005.

37. Author's interview with Leonard Cohen, Los Angeles, October 2005.

38. Author's interview with Leonard Cohen, Los Angeles, October 2005.

39. Page 82, *Various Positions.*

40. Published with permission of Leonard Cohen.

CHAPTER 7

41. Author's interview with Leonard Cohen, Los Angeles, October 2005.

42. Private letters of Marianne Ihlen.

43. Private letters of Marianne Ihlen.

44. Private letters of Marianne Ihlen.

45. Private letters of Marianne Ihlen.

CHAPTER 8

46. Private letters of Marianne Ihlen.

47. Private letters of Marianne Ihlen.

48. Private letters of Marianne Ihlen.

49. Private letters of Marianne Ihlen.

50. Private letters of Marianne Ihlen.

51. Private letters of Marianne Ihlen.

52. Private letters of Marianne Ihlen.

CHAPTER 9

53. Author's interview with Leonard Cohen, Los Angeles, October 2005.

CHAPTER 10

54. Private letters of Marianne Ihlen.

55. Author's interview with Leonard Cohen, Los Angeles, October 2005.

56. Author's interview with Leonard Cohen, Los Angeles, October 2005.

57. Published with permission of Leonard Cohen.

58. *Hjertets Kulturhistorie. Frå Antikken til i Dag.* Ole M. Høystad. Oslo: Spartacus, 2003.

59. Rembetiko, hash dens — *Bli Kjent med Hellas.* Ingunn Kvisterøy and Johan Henrik Schreiner. Oslo: Forlaget Hera, 1987.

60. Author's interview with Leonard Cohen, Los Angeles, October 2005.

61. Private letters of Marianne Ihlen.

62. Private letters of Marianne Ihlen.

CHAPTER 11

63 Private letters of Marianne Ihlen.

64. Page 107, *Various Positions.*

65. *Various Positions.*

66. Interview with Leonard Cohen, Los Angeles, October 2005.

67. Page 106, *Various Positions.*

68. Pages 83–84, *Various Positions.*

69. *Dictionary of Canadian Biography,* accessed on the internet at www.biographic.ca.

70. Author's interview with Leonard Cohen, Los Angeles, October 2005.

71. Author's interview with Leonard Cohen, Los Angeles, October 2005.

72. Author's interview with Leonard Cohen, Los Angeles, October 2005.

CHAPTER 12

73. Private letters of Marianne Ihlen.

74. Author's interview with Leonard Cohen, Los Angeles, October 2005.

75. Author's interview with Leonard Cohen, Los Angeles, October 2005.

76. Author's interview with Leonard Cohen, Los Angeles, October 2005.

77. Author's interview with Leonard Cohen, Los Angeles, October 2005.

78. Private letters of Marianne Ihlen.

79. Letters from Axel Jensen to Marianne Ihlen, and Wikipedia article on R.D. Laing, accessed on the internet at https://en.wikipedia.org/wiki/R._D._Laing.

80. Author's interview with Leonard Cohen, Los Angeles, October 2005.

81. Private letters of Marianne Ihlen.

82. Private letters of Marianne Ihlen.

83. Private letters of Marianne Ihlen.

84. Private letters of Marianne Ihlen.

85. Private letters of Leonard Cohen.

86. Page 241, *Charmian and George: the Marriage of George Johnston and Charmian Clift*. Max Brown. Sydney: Rosenberg Publishing, 2004.

87. Private letters of Marianne Ihlen.

88. Private papers of Marianne Ihlen.

89. Private letters of Marianne Ihlen.

CHAPTER 13

90. "Days of Kindness," © Leonard Cohen. *Stranger Music: Selected Poems and Songs*. Toronto: McClelland & Stewart, 1993.

SOURCES

This book is based primarily upon interviews and conversations with Marianne Ihlen as well as her private letters, notes and diaries from 1954 to 1972. The story also draws upon interviews with Leonard Cohen, undertaken during three days in Los Angeles in October 2005, and makes use of his private letters, unpublished poems and other material. Marianne Ihlen's and Axel Jensen's friends, Else Berit and Per Schioldborg, have contributed letters and information. Axel Jensen's widow, Prathiba Jensen, allowed me to quote from Axel's letters. Some material has been gathered from old newspaper articles in the archives of the National Library of Norway. A visit to Hydra together with Marianne in the autumn of 2007 was important for the story to come together.

Other sources that have provided information and inspiration:

The published works of Leonard Cohen, starting with his debut book, *Let Us Compare Mythologies* (Montreal: McGill Poetry Series, 1956), to his 2006 collection of poems, *Book of Longing* (Toronto: McClelland and Stewart).

Various Positions: A Life of Leonard Cohen. Ira B. Nadel. New York: Pantheon Books, 1996.

Ikaros. Axel Jensen. Oslo: Cappelen, 1957.

Line. Axel Jensen. Oslo: Cappelen, 1959.

Joachim. Axel Jensen. Oslo: Cappelen, 1961.

Trollmannen i Ålefjær. Axel Jensen om Axel Jensen. Jan Christan Mollestad. Oslo: Cappelen, 1993.

Axel Jensen. Livet Sett fra Nimbus. Petter Mejlænder. Oslo: Spartacus, 2002.

Hjertets Kulturhistorie. Frå Antikken til i Dag. Ole M. Høystad. Oslo: Spartacus, 2003.

Bli Kjent med Hellas. Ingunn Kvisterøy and Johan Henrik Schreiner. Oslo: Forlaget Hera, 1987.

Charmian and George: The Marriage of George Johnston and Charmian Clift. Max Brown. Sydney: Rosenberg, 2004.

Peel Me a Lotus. Charmian Clift. Hutchinson: London, 1959.

Ikke til Salgs. Melina Mercouri. Oslo: Gyldendal Norsk Forlag, 1971. (Originally published as *I Was Born Greek.* London: Hodder and Stoughton, 1971.)